Who Killed JFK?

Carl Oglesby

Odonian Press
Berkeley, California

Additional copies of this book and others in the Real Story series are available for $5 + $2 shipping per *order* (not per book) from Odonian Press, Box 7776, Berkeley CA 94707. For information on quantity discounts, please write or call us at 510/524-3143. Distribution to the book trade is through Publishers Group West, Box 8843, Emeryville CA 94662, 510/658-3453 (toll-free: 800/365-3453).

Main editor: Sandy Niemann

Developmental editor: Christine Carswell

Final editing, inside design, page layout, index:
Arthur Naiman

Cover photo: JFK in LA, June 1963, by Gene Daniels/
Black Star

Illustrations: John Grimes

Printing: Michelle Selby and Jim Puzey, Consolidated
Printers, Berkeley, California

Series editor: Arthur Naiman

Series coordinator: Susan McCallister

Printed in the United States of America

Printing # 1 2 3 4 5 6 7 8 9

Table of contents

Introduction

At about half past noon on November 22, 1963, John Fitzgerald Kennedy, the 35th president of the United States, was shot and killed while riding in a motorcade in Dallas, Texas. This book will prove to you that the official stories of what happened that day cannot possibly be true, that Kennedy was killed by a conspiracy and that the government of the United States has been—and still is—involved in covering up that conspiracy.

Chapter 1 discusses JFK's enemies and gives you some background on the events leading up to the fateful day. Chapter 2 gives the two official versions of what happened—by the Warren Commission (1964) and the House Select Committee on Assassinations (1979).

Chapter 3 presents overwhelming evidence that demolishes these official versions. Chapter 4 talks about who might have been involved in such a conspiracy, and discusses what we can do today to clear up the mystery.

When a public official is killed because some small group doesn't like his views, the people who voted for that public official are effectively disenfranchised. It is as if they never voted. So until we get to the bottom of the JFK assassination (and of the Robert Kennedy and Martin Luther King assassinations as well), and make sure that future assassinations can't happen, we have no right to say that we live in a democracy.

Chapter One

JFK's enemies

Although he has become a legend, John Fitzgerald Kennedy was hardly the most popular president in history when he was gunned down in November, 1963. In the previous six months alone, the Secret Service had reviewed over 400 threats to his life. Three of these were serious enough to entail changes in his security routine.

He was loathed by anti-Castro exiles, other right-wingers, the Mafia and even some of his own government agencies. In attempting to figure out who murdered him, it is important to understand who hated him, and why.

The stolen election

The seeds of that hatred were planted in the 1960 election that brought Kennedy to the presidency. The Democrats stole that election from Republican candidate Richard Nixon by tampering with the vote in two states. In Illinois, Mafia boss Sam Giancana arranged for 10,000 votes to be cast for John F. Kennedy "from the graveyard." In Texas, the political machine of Kennedy's running mate, Lyndon Johnson, arbitrarily disqualified about 100,000 votes.

As a result, 51 electoral votes that should have gone to Nixon went to Kennedy. Had they been added to Nixon's total, he would have squeezed into the presidency by one electoral vote.

Yet JFK quickly forgot his debts to Giancana and Johnson. Early in his presidency, he and his brother Robert established a special Justice Department strike force aimed at eradicating organized crime in the US. By the summer of 1963, JFK seemed ready to dump Johnson from his 1964 reelection ticket because Johnson's long-time personal secretary, Bobby Baker, had been implicated in a scandal involving federal farm subsidies.

The Bay of Pigs

Soon after the 1960 election, JFK made new enemies. In 1960, President Eisenhower's last year in office, a force of 1400 anti-Communist Cuban exiles was assembled to overthrow Fidel Castro. JFK allowed this force to invade Cuba in April 1961. But when it landed at the Bay of Pigs, it found it had underestimated the extent of Castro's support.

Pinned down on the beach, the invaders appealed to Kennedy for US air and naval support. He refused, leaving them to be taken prisoner by Castro's forces. This embittered all those involved in the anti-Castro cause, including the Mafia, which wanted its Cuban casinos back.

Kennedy then retaliated against those in the CIA he felt had misled him about the strength of anti-Castro sympathy in Cuba. He told a high official that he would "splinter the CIA in a thousand pieces and scatter it to the winds." His purge removed CIA Director Allen Dulles, Deputy Director General Charles

Cabell (the brother of the mayor of Dallas) and Deputy Director of Plans Richard Bissell.

Kennedy went on to ransom the Bay of Pigs prisoners for tractors, and promised them another try at overthrowing Castro. Then, in October 1962, he surrounded Cuba with a naval blockade and forced Soviet leader Nikita Khrushchev to remove his missiles. After the Missile Crisis (as it was called), JFK abandoned the anti-Castro movement altogether. He closed its training bases in Florida and Louisiana, promised the USSR he would respect Cuba's sovereignty and began to negotiate for improved relations with Castro himself.

The USSR

Needless to say, JFK's handling of the Cuban situation did nothing to win over the right wing, nor Kennedy's critics in the military. He further alienated them in his relations with the USSR.

Khrushchev's reading of the Bay of Pigs "fiasco" (as it came to be called) was that JFK was an ineffectual leader who could easily be pushed around. This point of view was reinforced by JFK's failure to react when, in 1961, the Soviet Union built a wall across Berlin, dividing the city, and threatened to attack the Western allies if they stayed there.

JFK did "stand up to the Russians" during the Missile Crisis but then, less than a year later, he signed a limited nuclear test-ban treaty with Moscow, which made the right wing think that he accepted Communist control over Eastern Europe and the Baltic States and was surrendering in the Cold War.

The Vietnam War

Even worse, by the fall of 1963, JFK was ready to cut his losses and pull out of Vietnam. Since South Vietnam's government was so unpopular, Kennedy saw no chance of a US victory without an impossibly large commitment of resources. He sent a high-level fact-finding mission to Vietnam, and it proposed the withdrawal of 1000 US troops by the end of the year and the phase-out of US military forces by the end of 1965.

Kennedy's critics believed that his endorsement of this proposal virtually guaranteed that the whole of Southeast Asia would fall to the Communists.

The civil rights movement

For all these reasons, Kennedy had infuriated the right throughout the country. But what particularly galled those in the South was his encouragement of the civil rights movement.

In October 1962, JFK sent federal marshals and troops to force the integration of the University of Mississippi. In the summer of 1963, he supported a bill that would guarantee the right to vote and access to all public accommodations for every citizen, regardless of color—the most aggressive legislative attack on segregation since the Civil War.

The trip to Texas

Given the number of JFK's enemies—the CIA, the Mafia, anti-Castro Cubans, the Republicans, southern racists, the military and even his own vice-president—and all the threats against his life, it is hardly surprising that Kennedy's proposed trip to Texas in the fall of 1963 was hotly debated within the White House.

Texas, and Dallas in particular, were strongholds of the far right. There was even some chance that the entire Texas Democratic party might bolt to the Republicans in the 1964 election—especially if Johnson were dumped from the ticket.

Virtually everyone in the Texas Democratic party— from conservatives like LBJ and Governor John Connally to liberals like Senator Ralph Yarborough— argued that Kennedy had to come down and face his critics personally. But other advisers were not so sure. Given the mood of the state, a trip to Texas seemed too risky.

Only three weeks before, Adlai Stevenson, Kennedy's ambassador to the United Nations, had been manhandled by a hostile crowd in Dallas. On November 4, a Texan member of the National Democratic Committee, Byron Selton, wrote Robert Kennedy that a prominent Dallas businessman called JFK "a liability to the free world" and urged that the trip to Texas, or at least the Dallas leg of it, be cancelled.

But if he didn't go, would he lose the Democrats in Texas? And if he lost them there, what would happen in the rest of the South? How could he hope to win reelection in 1964? So he decided that he and Jackie would take a two-day trip to Texas, visiting San Antonio, Houston, Fort Worth and Dallas.

All went well on the first day, and the mood on the tour was increasingly up-beat when it reached Dallas on the morning of November 22. The rightist protestors were certainly visible—the *Dallas Morning News* hit the streets that Friday with a full page ad in which such Texas business figures as Nelson Bunker Hunt accused JFK of caving in to "the Spirit of Moscow." The ad held JFK responsible for the imprisonment of thousands of anti-Castro Cubans, charged him with selling food to Vietnamese Communists, and claimed that he had cut a secret deal with the US Communist Party.

All along the motorcade route, John Birch volunteers distributed a leaflet showing a front view and profile of JFK, like a police mug shot, with the title *Wanted for Treason*. It spelled out seven ways in which JFK was guilty of "treasonous activities against the United States."

But the protestors were vastly outnumbered by the cheering thousands who turned out on that bright, clear day to welcome the Kennedys. As the motorcade left downtown and entered Dealey Plaza, Governor Connally's wife, Nellie, obviously relieved that things were going so well, turned around in her jump seat in front of Jackie and said, "Well, Mr. President, you can't say the people of Dallas don't love you."

JFK smiled. "Obviously," he said. An instant later, shots were fired. "My God, I've got his brains in my hand," Connally recalls Jackie wailing as the president slumped dead in her arms.

Within an hour, Dallas policeman J.D. Tippit was shot down blocks away. Two days later, the man accused of murdering both men, Lee Harvey Oswald, was himself murdered while in police custody by Jack Ruby.

Chapter Two

The official versions of what happened

How many shots were fired in Dealey Plaza? Where did they come from? Who really fired them? Was there more than one gunman? Rumor and speculation exploded throughout the world.

As Deputy Attorney General Nicholas Katzenbach wrote Chief Justice Earl Warren on December 9, 1963: "The latest Gallup poll shows that over half the American people believe that Oswald acted as part of a conspiracy in shooting President Kennedy, and there is considerable rumor in this country and abroad to the effect that Ruby acted as part of the same or a related conspiracy."

"The thing I am concerned about," FBI boss J. Edgar Hoover wrote in a memo to President Johnson on November 24, "and so is Mr. Katzenbach, is having something issued so we can convince the public that Oswald is the real assassin."

Johnson moved quickly to assemble a special presidential commission and to staff it with the most credible political figures possible. Within seven days after the shooting, he appointed Democrats Richard B. Russell of Georgia and Hale Boggs of Louisiana, Republicans John Sherman Cooper of Kentucky and Gerald Ford of Michigan, former CIA director Allen W. Dulles, and John J. McCloy, who had been president of the World Bank and also US High Commissioner for Germany—all men of prestige and high public trust.

He had to use all his powers of persuasion to get the Chief Justice of the Supreme Court, Earl Warren, to become chairman. "I felt that we needed a Republican chairman whose judicial ability and fairness were unquestioned," Johnson explained in his memoir, *The Vantage Point*. Warren's reputation, Johnson thought, would give the commission's findings national and worldwide credibility.

And so the President's Commission on the Assassination of the President became known as the Warren Commission. By the end of January 1964, its staff was assembled. Its hearings began on February 3. It heard testimony from 552 witnesses. On June 17, it finished gathering its evidence and began drafting its 888-page report, which it presented to President Johnson on September 24. Shortly afterwards, the commission published 15 volumes of testimony and 11 volumes of exhibits.

The Warren Commission's version

Here's the story of the JFK assassination as the Warren Commission presented it:

Friday, November 22, 1963, 11:55 am: The presidential motorcade left Air Force 1 at Love Field in Dallas for the Trade Mart downtown. There, JFK was to deliver one last speech to a group of businessmen before flying back to Washington.

The presidential limousine convertible had been flown ahead, as was routine, by the Secret Service. JFK and Jackie sat in the rear seat—JFK on the right and Jackie on his left. In front of JFK on a jumpseat was John Connally, and to his left, in front of Jackie, was Nellie Connally.

12:30 pm: Led by an unmarked Dallas police car half a block ahead, the JFK motorcade entered Dealey Plaza, which was at the end of the parade route. The crowd was massive along the preceding mile but only 70 people were in the Plaza.

The motorcade headed east to west on Main Street, then turned north up Houston Street and finally turned sharply southwest in a 120-degree turn onto Elm Street, bringing it directly in front of the Texas School Book Depository. As the presidential limousine drove away from the Depository, traveling about 8–10 mph, shots were fired.

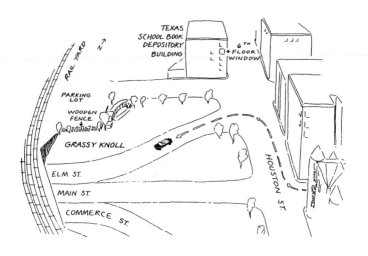

Dealey Plaza in Dallas, where JFK was shot

The Warren Commission stated that there were three: one that hit the curb well in front of the limousine; another that hit the president's back, came out through his neck and hit Connally below the right armpit; and the fatal one that hit the president in the head. The commission said it could not determine the exact sequence of these shots, stating only that the shot that struck both JFK and Connally came before the fatal head shot.

Secret Service, FBI and Dallas Police Department determinations of the exact time of the gunfire vary from 12:30–12:35. The duration of the gunfire, however, is known to have been between 4.8 and 7.9 seconds.

Much of the Warren Commission's detailed knowledge of the shooting was thanks to Abraham Zapruder, an admirer of JFK's, who had recently bought an eight-millimeter Bell & Howell camera to record the president's visit. Zapruder was waiting to film the motorcade on a five-foot cement block at the top of a grassy knoll that rises toward a pergola and picket fence, behind which there are a parking lot and railroad yard.

From the moment the president's limousine turned onto Elm Street (seconds before the shooting began) until it disappeared under the overpass to his right, Zapruder filmed the motorcade—creating what was to become probably the most important home movie in history.

Even though the gunfire shocked Zapruder (there is a jolt in his filming), he never let the limousine out of his sight—except for eight-tenths of a second when a road sign obstructed the view. But this was exactly when one shot was fired. When JFK disappeared behind the road sign, he was not hit yet; when he reappeared, he was clearly reacting to a wound in his throat.

One other person was hit in the Dealey Plaza shooting: a spectator named James Tague, who was standing on the south side of Elm Street near the overpass. One of the shots struck the curbstone several feet in front of him, and a fragment of either stone or bullet wounded him slightly in the cheek.

12:31–12.32 pm: Dallas police officer Marrion Baker was on his motorcycle seven cars back in the motorcade when the shots were fired. His spontaneous impression was that the shots had been fired from high up in the Book Depository. He immediately drove up to the building, left his motorcycle and ran up to the main entrance. There he encountered the building superintendent, Roy Truly, and the two of them ran into the building.

In the employees' lunchroom on the second floor, Baker, with his revolver drawn, confronted the only person in the room—Lee Harvey Oswald, standing at the soft-drinks machine.

Baker and Truly later testified that Oswald was calm—not winded, armed or behaving suspiciously. Baker asked Truly who Oswald was, and Truly told him that he was a building employee. Baker then ran up to the roof of the building with Truly.

12:33 pm: A minute later, Oswald left the Book Depository by the front entrance. The police would soon seal the building, round up the employees and discover that Oswald was missing.

Oswald walked east on Elm for four-tenths of a mile, boarded a public bus, left it when it stalled in traffic, walked south two blocks and finally took a cab to a point a half mile from his rooming house at 1026 North Beckley Street in the Oak Cliff section of Dallas, about two-and-a-half miles away from Dealey Plaza. There he picked up his revolver, a Smith & Wesson .38.

12:36 pm: The presidential limousine arrived at Parkland Hospital's emergency entrance. Kennedy and Connally were immediately wheeled into trauma rooms where medical teams awaited them.

12:44 pm: Oswald's description, but not his name, was put out over the police radio: "the suspect...is supposed to be an unknown white male, approximately 30, 165 pounds, slender build, armed with what is thought to be a 30-30 rifle."

1:00 pm: Parkland Hospital doctors informed the Secret Service and Lyndon Johnson that President Kennedy was dead.

1:10 pm: Deputy Sheriff Luke Mooney, searching the southeast corner of the sixth floor of the Book Depository, noticed a creased box propped in the window. Looking closer, he saw three spent cartridge cases. He leaned out the window and called down to the Dallas County Sheriff Bill Decker and Dallas Police Captain Will Fritz that he had discovered what appeared to be a sniper's nest made out of book boxes.

1:15 pm: Dallas patrolman J.D. Tippit stopped a pedestrian, later said to be Oswald, a little less than a mile south of Oswald's rooming house. Without reporting first over his radio, Tippit left the car to confront the pedestrian, who, apparently without provocation or an exchange of words, fatally shot Tippit four times in the head, chest and stomach with a .38-caliber revolver.

Tippit's assailant left the scene at a trot, reloading his revolver and dropping casings as he went. An unidentified male called the police over Tippit's radio to report that Tippit had been shot dead: "We've had a shooting here...it's a police officer, somebody shot him." The police clock fixed 1:16 as the time of Tippit's death.

1:20 pm: The Secret Service put the bubble top and canvas cover on the death limousine and had it flown back to Washington.

1:22 pm: A 6.5-mm Mannlicher-Carcano bolt-action rifle was found behind some boxes in the northwest corner of the sixth floor of the Book Depository. Its serial number was traced to A. Hidell, an alias Oswald had been using since his days in the Marines.

1:40 pm: Six-tenths of a mile from the scene of the Tippit shooting and 24 minutes later, a shoe salesman standing at the curb near his store saw a man sneak into the Texas Theater without a ticket. The salesman and an usher entered the theater to look for the suspicious man while the box office cashier called the police.

Within five minutes, 24 policemen descended in squad cars. They sealed the exits, put on the lights, and easily spotted, challenged and overpowered Oswald, who was sitting alone in the middle of the main floor. Oswald drew his revolver but was subdued before firing.

2:00 pm: Parkland Hospital senior engineer Darrell C. Tomlinson was pushing a stretcher out of the way in the hospital basement when a slug rolled out from under the mattress.

Later dubbed "the magic bullet" because of its pristine condition and its strange flight path (as we shall see), it became Commission Exhibit 399. The Warren Commission claimed it was the first bullet that hit Kennedy—the one that went through his body and then hit John Connally.

2:10 pm: Oswald was brought to the homicide office of the Dallas Police Department where he was soon identified by Patrolman Marrion Baker as the man he had seen in the lunchroom of the Book Depository.

2:38 pm: LBJ was sworn in as president on Air Force 1. Within ten minutes, the aircraft took off for Washington with JFK's body on board—en route to Bethesda Naval Hospital where seven to nine hours after the assassination (accounts of the time vary), the autopsy would begin.

3:10–4:00 pm: Homicide captain Will Fritz and FBI agents James Hosty and James Bookhout conducted the first interrogation of Oswald. His attitude, according to Bookhout, was "very arrogant and argumentative." Hosty said Oswald was extremely hostile. Amazingly, no transcript or any other written or taped record of this or subsequent interrogations of Oswald was kept.

4:05–4:20 pm: Oswald was presented, along with three others, in the first of three line-ups before witnesses to the Tippit shooting. He was then interrogated for the second time. Using information about Oswald's past obtained from the FBI, Captain Fritz questioned Oswald about his travels to the Soviet Union and Mexico City.

According to Fritz, Oswald admitted having been to the Soviet Union but denied traveling to Mexico City the previous month, denied owning a rifle and claimed that he had been eating lunch inside the Depository Building when JFK was shot.

6:20–6:37 pm: Oswald was taken from his second interrogation to his second line-up. As he left the line-up, he was questioned by reporters in the hall. He expressed surprise to hear that Governor Connally had been shot.

7:10 pm: Oswald was formally told that he was charged with the murder of Patrolman Tippit. According to FBI agent Hosty, Oswald "emphatically denied" any role in the Kennedy or Tippit murder.

Midnight: At the request of reporters, the police arranged a 5-10 minute press conference in the police assembly room, presenting Oswald for direct questioning for the first time. He denied any knowledge of killing anyone, saying bitterly, "I'm just the patsy." Jack Ruby was in the crowd.

Saturday, November 23, 1:35 am: Oswald was formally charged with killing the president.

10:35–11:30 am: Oswald was again interviewed by Fritz and representatives of the FBI and Secret Service. Although FBI agent Bookhout characterized Oswald as "less belligerent" than he had been the day before, he still refused to discuss certain points, such as the Selective Service draft card he had been found carrying, signed in his hand Alek J. Hidell. He also refused to take a polygraph test.

6:30–7:30 pm: Interviewed yet again, Oswald was shown a set of photographs the police said they had found among his belongings—photos showing Oswald wearing a holstered pistol and carrying a rifle in one hand and publications of the US Communist Party and the Socialist Workers Party in the other. Oswald insisted he had never seen them before, and that they had been forged by superimposing his face on the body of someone else.

Sunday, November 24, 11:20 am: Oswald was to be transferred from the city jail to the Dallas County jail, as was routine with murder suspects. The police notified the media that the transfer would take place sometime after ten o'clock Sunday morning. Earlier that morning, between 2:30 and 3:00 am, two anonymous calls threatening Oswald's life had been received, one by the Dallas FBI and the other by the county sheriff, but the police decided to go ahead with the transfer as planned.

At 11:20, Oswald, in handcuffs and with detectives on either side and behind him but no one in front, emerged from the jail basement. He was led through a loading area toward an unmarked police car. In the words of the Warren Commission Report :

> [Oswald] took a few steps toward the car and was in the glaring light of the television cameras when a man suddenly darted out from an area on the right of the cameras where newsmen had been assembled. The man was carrying a Colt .38 revolver in his right hand and, while millions watched on television, he moved quickly to within a few feet of Oswald and fired one shot into Oswald's abdomen. Oswald groaned with pain as he fell to the ground and quickly lost consciousness. Within seven minutes Oswald was at Parkland Hospital where, without having regained consciousness, he was pronounced dead at 1:07 pm.

The man who shot and killed Oswald was Jack Ruby, owner and manager of Dallas's Carousel nightclub. When questioned immediately afterwards, Ruby "denied that the killing of Oswald was in any way connected with a conspiracy involving the assassination of President Kennedy. He maintained that he had done it in a temporary fit of depression and rage over the president's death."

The Warren Commission agreed completely. It concluded that Oswald was one lone nut and Ruby another. There was no conspiracy.

The House Committee's version

The Warren Commission hoped its report would bring the question of JFK's killer to a close. But from the beginning there were doubts about its findings. A Harris Poll taken shortly after the Warren Report was published showed that 31% of Americans still believed Oswald was not alone and that more than half believed that the Warren Commission had failed to find and tell the whole story.

Between 1964 and 1967, at least nine books critical of the lone-assassin theory were published. By 1967, 64% of Americans believed in a conspiracy. In the 1970s the percentage grew still larger, fueled by a Senate Intelligence Committee investigation of two pieces of evidence that had been withheld from the Warren Commission.

The first, leaked by an anonymous source in the FBI, was a letter Oswald hand-delivered to agent James Hosty at the FBI office on November 6. Hosty was responsible for maintaining the FBI file on Oswald. The Bureau was keeping an eye on Oswald, it claimed, because he was a Castro supporter and was married to a Soviet citizen.

Hosty had been extensively questioned by the Warren Commission but chose to say nothing about the letter Oswald had given him. Nor did he reveal that, a few hours after Ruby had killed Oswald, his supervisor at the FBI, Gordon Shanklin, had ordered that Oswald's letter be destroyed. Hosty had torn it up and flushed it down the office toilet. (As a result of this revelation, Hosty was suspended from the FBI for several months.)

The second was a list made public in 1975 by Fidel Castro of "about thirty" attempts on his life—all, he thought, traceable to the CIA. Upon investigation, the Senate Intelligence Committee discovered that the CIA had indeed masterminded assassination plots against many foreign leaders, and had teamed up with the Mafia on several occasions.

The committee reasoned that these plots were relevant to the Kennedy assassination because Castro might have hired Oswald (given his alleged Communist sympathies) to retaliate against the US by assassinating JFK, and it sharply criticized several former CIA officials—especially commission member and former CIA chief Allen Dulles—for not informing the Warren Commission about them.

These new revelations, coupled with the ever-lingering doubts about the Warren Commission findings, renewed public interest in the JFK case, and the House Select Committee on Assassinations was formed.

Until almost the end of its investigations, late in 1978, it seemed that the committee would virtually repeat the Warren Commission's claim that there were three shots at Dealey Plaza and that all of them were fired by Oswald. The one new possibility the committee entertained was that the Mafia might have backed Oswald (since his uncle, Charles "Dutz" Murret of New Orleans, was a low-level operative in the Marcello crime family).

But just when the committee's conclusions seemed certain, the new acoustics evidence (discussed in detail in Chapter 3) was introduced. It indicated that there had actually been four shots, and that one was fired from the grassy knoll in front of the motorcade.

This compelled the committee to revise its opinion. While still agreeing with the Warren Commission that the fatal head shot had come from behind and that Oswald had fired it, the committee was forced to conclude that a second gunman—whose shot, in its view, missed—had also fired at JFK from the front, and that this suggested a "probable conspiracy."

Although the report stopped short of naming those responsible for the conspiracy, it indicated suspicion of the Cuban corner of the Mafia and possibly the Cuban corner of the CIA.

But, instead of fostering a new national dedication to solving the case, the committee disbanded at the end of the 95th Congressional session and the matter was dropped. Why?

First, even though the committee's final report was undoubtedly shocking to some, Congress failed to build a political consensus for carrying the investigation further. Second, the Reagan era was about to begin and his attorney general, Ed Meese, was disinclined to renew an investigation of a 20-year-old murder of the Democratic Party's fallen hero.

Third, in 1982, the National Academy of Sciences questioned the acoustics evidence and decided that what had been interpreted as gun shots might not have been shots at all—thus casting doubt upon the key piece of evidence leading to the committee's new conclusions. The Justice Department, under Meese, was quick to reassert that the Warren Commission findings were correct—a lone assassin had killed President Kennedy.

Chapter Three

Evidence of a conspiracy

There are three main areas in which not only the Warren Commission's lone-assassin theory but also the House Assassinations Committee findings are inadequate. First, a large body of evidence indicates that at least two gunmen fired at Kennedy. One of these gunmen, who appears to have fired the fatal head shot, was on the grassy knoll to JFK's front and right.

Second, another body of evidence, less definite but nevertheless powerful, indicates that Oswald was not one of those two or three gunmen at all, but was, as he put it, "the patsy." He certainly was not the lone nut the Warren Report suggested. On the contrary, Oswald was connected to official intelligence bodies as well as to a New Orleans-based group of anti-Castro militants which seems to have been either an illegal creation of rogue elements of the CIA or a CIA spin-off.

Third, there is strong evidence that Jack Ruby was not a lone nut either, and that he did not kill Oswald out of some muddled personal impulse but was ordered to do so, to prevent the trial in which Oswald might successfully have defended himself.

The single-bullet theory

The Warren Commission's lone-assassin theory rests on the belief that there were three shots, all of them fired by one man from the Book Depository behind the president.

To sustain it, the commission had to explain two things. The first was Abraham Zapruder's 22-second movie of the event, which indicated a gap of a half second to a second between JFK's reaction to the shot to his throat and Connally's reaction to the shot to his back.

The second was the performance capability of the 6.5-mm Mannlicher-Carcano rifle which was found in the Book Depository, which Oswald had bought eight months before from a mail-order house for $21.45 (including postage) and which the Warren Commission claimed he used to shoot the president.

This was a clumsy, bolt-action rifle used by the Italian army in the early days of World War II. Oswald's particular rifle was adjudged especially stiff—tests conducted by Warren Commission experts established a minimum refiring time of 2.3 seconds.

Then how could Connally have been hit a half second to a second after JFK if only Oswald was firing? The Mannlicher-Carcano could not be refired that quickly. The only solution—and the one the Warren Commission adopted—was the so-called single-bullet theory: that one shot must have been responsible for the wounds to both men.

In this theory, a bullet hit Kennedy in the back, came out at his neck, changed direction, hit Connally in the right armpit, blew out a five-inch section of a rib upon exiting, went through his right wrist from back to front, breaking it into several pieces, and pierced his left thigh.

From the beginning there were doubts about this single-bullet theory. Three of the Warren commissioners—one shy of a majority—did not believe it even as they put their names to the report presenting it.

Georgia Senator Richard Russell wanted a footnote on the single-bullet theory indicating that he did not accept it, but Warren overruled him. Kentucky Senator Sherman Cooper told a writer, "I, too, objected to such a conclusion; there was no evidence to show both men were hit by the same bullet." Louisiana Congressman Hale Boggs "also had strong doubts."

The medical panel of the 1978 House Assassinations Committee concurred: "The medical evidence alone does not provide the panel with sufficient information to state with absolute certainty that the bullet that struck Governor Connally was the same one which had previously struck President Kennedy."

The problems with this theory are greater than either the Warren Commission members or the Assassinations Committee report suggests. First, how could Connally hold his rather heavy Stetson hat in his right hand after the bullet had already smashed his right wrist?

The Warren Commission theorized that this was possible because Connally "didn't immediately feel the penetration of the bullet, then felt the delayed reaction of the impact on his back." But this ignored the testimony of Dr. Robert Shaw, the Parkland surgeon who treated Connally's chest wounds. Shaw told the commission that "in the case of a wound which strikes a bony substance such as a rib, usually the reaction is quite prompt."

Second, Kennedy's and Connally's wounds do not begin to line up, despite the commission's attempt to make them seem to do so. The bullet holes in the back of Kennedy's jacket and shirt are five and three-quarter inches below the collar and slightly to the right of the spine, corresponding exactly with the location recorded on the autopsy diagram made at Bethesda.

But the wound in the front of his neck is several inches higher in his body, at the area of the knot in his necktie. If the back and throat wounds are connected as entrance and exit, and JFK was sitting erect when hit (as his back brace required and as the photographs display), then the bullet must have coursed slightly upwards through his body and exited on an upwards slant and in a right-to-left direction.

Such a trajectory would have carried the bullet up and out of the car to the left, away from Connally, who, from the perspective of a Book Depository sniper, was positioned somewhat to JFK's right. In contrast, the entrance wound in Connally's right armpit was several inches lower and to the right of JFK's neck wound.

A bullet can indeed change its trajectory after it hits flesh, loses its spin and begins to tumble, but the deflection required to connect the pathway of JFK's back wound with that of Connally's is highly unlikely—especially since the distance between the two men was only about 28 inches.

Third, the experienced trauma-room surgeons who first examined the president at Parkland Hospital in Dallas minutes after the shooting interpreted the wound in the front of his throat as one of entrance rather than exit—it was small, neat and had the "sucking" appearance characteristic of entry wounds. (The Parkland doctors did not turn the body over and therefore did not see the wound in the back. Later, at Bethesda, this wound was described as shallow, no deeper than the first joint of the doctor's little finger.)

Dr. Kemp Clark, who pronounced Kennedy dead, was quoted in the November 27 *New York Times* as saying that one bullet struck Kennedy "about the necktie knot. It ranged downward in his chest and didn't exit." That same day, the *New York Herald-Tribune* quoted Dr. Robert Shaw as saying that a bullet entered the front of the president's throat and "coursed downward into his lung."

But because the Parkland doctors had to enlarge the throat wound in a tracheotomy when they attempted to resuscitate the president, their definition of it as one of entrance rather than exit depended solely upon their immediate subjective impressions. So the Warren Commission chose to disregard their statements and to claim instead that the neck wound was a wound of exit, made by the bullet that entered the president's back.

Fourth, this single bullet (known as CE—for "Commission Exhibit"—399, or the "magic bullet") is alleged to have wounded both the president and the Governor, yet emerged from the experience in a nearly pristine condition—as though it might have been fired into a tub of water or a bale of cotton.

It was slightly compressed at its base but otherwise undeformed. It lacked less than three grains from its original 161-grain weight and showed none of the severe distortion expected of a bullet fired through bone. The Warren Report called it "nearly whole."

Despite this incongruity, the House Committee did not conduct the relatively simple and inexpensive ballistics tests that might have shown whether it was physically possible for a Mannlicher-Carcano bullet to cause the damage the single-bullet theory imputes to it while undergoing as little deformation as did bullet CE 399.

What's more, there was far too much lead in Connally's body for it to have been deposited by a bullet emerging "nearly whole." Audrey Bell, the head nurse in the trauma room where Connally was treated

The bullet above was fired into a cadaver's wristbone. Note how flattened the tip is.

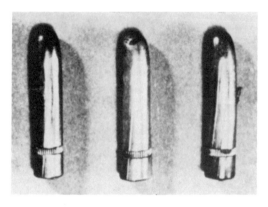

Both the outside bullets above were fired into tubes of cotton. The middle one is CE 399, the "magic bullet," which the Warren Commission says passed through JFK's body, changed course and shattered one of Governor Connally's ribs and his right wrist. Note how much more it looks like the bullets on either side of it than the one at the top of the page.

(and who was not interviewed by the Warren Commission), told House Assassinations Committee investigators that she was given four or five fragments from Connally's right wrist, and that she put them into an envelope and turned them over to the FBI.

In 1978, Bell told British author Anthony Summers that "The smallest [of these fragments] was the size of the striking end of a match and the largest at least twice that big. I have seen a picture of the magic bullet, and I can't see how it could be the bullet from which the fragments I saw came."

Charles Harbison, a Texas State Highway patrolman also ignored by the Warren Commission, told the House Committee that he had turned over to the FBI three additional bullet fragments that fell from Connally's leg when he helped move Connally to another hospital room three or four days after the shooting.

If these seven or eight fragments were deposited by a single bullet that passed through Connally's body, then CE 399 could not have been this bullet and the single-bullet theory collapses on this point alone.

Fifth, and perhaps most compelling, John Connally himself testified against the single-bullet theory soon after the event. He has restated his story without variance down the decades and is supported in its details by his wife, Nellie, who saw it all from the adjacent seat.

In 1966, Connally told the editors of *Life* magazine, who were then critical of the Warren Report and calling for a new investigation:

Between the time I heard the first shot and felt the impact of the other bullet that obviously hit me, I sensed something was wrong and said, "Oh, no, no, no." After I felt the impact, I glanced down and saw that my whole chest was covered with blood....

When I heard that first shot and was starting to turn to my right to see what happened, Nellie saw the president's hands reaching for his throat. I started to look around over my left shoulder, and somewhere in that revolution I was hit. My recollection of that time gap, the distinct separation between the shot that hit the president and the impact of the one that hit me, is as clear today as it was then....

They talk about the one-bullet or two-bullet theory, but as far as I'm concerned, there's no "theory." There's my absolute knowledge, and Nellie's too, that one bullet caused the president's first wound and that an entirely separate shot struck me.

Nellie Connally also shared her recollections with *Life:*

As far as the first two shots go, my memory is divided into four distinct events. First I heard the shot, or a strange loud noise—I'm not that expert on rifles—back behind us. Then next I turned to my right and saw the president gripping at his throat. Then I turned back toward John, and I heard the second shot that hit John....

I must have been looking right at him when it hit because I saw him recoil to the right....So you see I had time to look at the president *after* he was already hit, then turn and see John hit by a second shot.

Nellie Connally added, "No one will ever convince me otherwise." And her husband agreed, "It's a certainty. I'll never change my mind."

The Warren Commission attempted to analyze away the Connallys' testimony but never directly confronted the fact that it contradicted the single-bullet theory. The single-bullet theory does not appear to be a credible interpretation of the facts.

The witnesses

If different bullets hit Connally and JFK, and Oswald could not have fired again so quickly using a Mannlicher-Carcano rifle, then there must have been at least one other gunman.

Where might he have been positioned? Several different kinds of evidence, including the testimony of a great many eyewitnesses, suggest that at least one shot came from in front of the president.

Of the 178 witnesses in Dealey Plaza who gave statements to the Warren Commission and who had an opinion on the direction of the shots, 49 believed they came from the Texas School Book Depository behind the presidential limousine and 61 believed that at least one of the shots was fired from in front. The Warren Commission chose to believe the smaller group.

The following statements from witnesses either in the motorcade or in the grassy knoll area are typical of those rejected by the Warren Commission:

Secret Service Agent Forrest Sorrels, traveling in the lead car just ahead of the limousine: "I looked toward the top of the terrace to my right as the sounds of the shots seemed to come from that direction."

Secret Service Agent Paul Landis in the car behind the limousine: "I heard a second report and saw the president's head split open and pieces of flesh and blood flying through the air. My reaction at this time was that the shot came from somewhere toward the front."

David F. Powers, a top JFK aide, was riding in the Secret Service car immediately behind the presidential limousine. He filed an affidavit with the Warren Commission in which he said, "My first impression was that the shots came from the right and overhead, but I also had a fleeting impression that the noise appeared to come from the front in the area of the triple overpass." In 1976 he told an interviewer, "I remember ducking my head as if a flash came from the right front."

Eleven-year-veteran police officer B. J. Martin and nine-year-veteran Bobby W. Hargis were on their motorcycles directly to the left and rear of the limousine. Both were splattered with blood. Hargis told the Warren Commission that he "was next to Mrs. Kennedy when I heard the first shot....the [next] bullet [hit] him in the head, the one that killed him and it seemed like his head exploded, and I was splattered with blood and brain, and kind of a bloody water."

Hargis was unsure of the direction of the shots but told the commission, "there was something in my head that said that they probably could have been coming from the railroad overpass...since I got splattered with blood...."

Of the dozen or so witnesses who were either in the line of fire between the grassy knoll and JFK or on the overpass, almost all believed that some of the shots were fired from higher up on the knoll:

William Newman, a Korean War combat veteran standing near the north curb of Elm Street and roughly in the line of fire from the limo to the grassy knoll, said: "I thought the shot had come from the garden directly behind me, that it was on an elevation from where I was right on the curb. Then we fell down on the grass as it seemed we were in the direct path of fire."

Gordon Arnold, a 22-year-old soldier alert to the sounds of live ammunition, was standing high on the knoll west of the colonnade. "The shot came from behind me," he said, "only inches over my left shoulder. I had just got out of basic training. In my mind, live ammunition was being fired. It was being fired over my head. And I hit the dirt."

Sam Holland, a railroad signal supervisor, was watching from the overpass. He told the police that shots were fired from "behind that picket fence— close to the little plaza—there's no doubt whatsoever in my mind."

Luke Winborn was on the overpass. In 1966 he told a private investigator that "the smoke hung in the trees" at the crest of the grassy knoll.

Lee Bowers, another railroad worker, was in the 14-foot signal tower 50 yards north of the fence at the top of the grassy knoll. He noticed two men on the north side of the fence just before the shooting, "the only two strangers in the area." At the moment of the shooting and "in the vicinity of where the two men I have described were, there was a flash of light...or smoke or something which caused me to feel that something out of the ordinary had occurred there."

JFK's reaction

The most powerful evidence that a shot was fired from the front and the right of the president is the Zapruder film itself. There we see JFK clutch his throat and slowly topple forward and to his left into Jackie's arms. About five seconds go by.

Then the president's head explodes and a cloud of red mist suddenly surrounds the back of the car. A flap of skin peels off the right side of his head and his head snaps backward, seeming to pull his body back into the seat.

In a slowed-down, optically-enhanced version of the film produced by technical expert Robert Groden, we can see bits of brain tissue and fragments of bone being flung out behind and to the left of the car. Jackie scrambles onto the trunk of the limo reaching for a bone fragment until secret service-man Roy Kellerman leaps up to help her back into her seat. Then William Greer, the limousine driver, hits the accelerator.

How could a shot fired from the sixth floor of the Book Depository 260 feet behind and above JFK have had this result? Why would his head snap backward or bits of brain tissue fly out behind the car if he had been hit from the rear?

As Dr. R.A.J. Riddle of the UCLA Brain Institute says, "Newton's second law of motion has remained inviolate for three centuries. No physical phenomenon is known that fails to obey it....Thus if someone is shot, and the shot strikes home, the general direction of recoil will be away from—not toward—the marksman."

The defenders of the Warren Commission developed numerous theories to explain away the president's reaction. First, they speculated that the car had suddenly accelerated just at the moment of the head shot, and that this sudden acceleration had jerked Kennedy's head backwards. But the Zapruder film showed that the car was in fact slowing down at the moment of impact and that no one else in it showed any sign of backward movement.

Then the commission developed a second theory: a "jet effect" was involved in which the bullet, impacting from behind, explosively compressed the brain within the skull. The brain then blew out the front of the president's head, driving it backwards.

But the Zapruder film, eye witnesses and medical testimony all reveal that the debris was blown out of the back of the head, not the front. Moreover, the gaping five-inch head wound of exit described by the trauma-room medical people (see below) was in the back, not in the front.

The House Assassinations Committee adopted a third theory: the shot to the brain triggered a "neuromuscular reaction," a kind of whole-body seizure which then created the false impression of a shot from the front.

This theory was adopted even though expert testimony stated that the proposed neuromuscular reaction "usually does not commence for several minutes after separation of the upper brain centers from the brain stem and spinal cord." Moreover, the Zapruder film showed that the body did not stiffen but was thrown like a rag doll into the back of the seat at an acceleration calculated at 80–100 feet per second.

The medical evidence

Those present at Trauma Room One at Parkland Hospital, Dallas, unanimously concluded that the president had been fatally struck from "in front as he faced the assailant," to quote Dr. Malcolm Perry.

All observed a massive wound in the back of the president's head. Dr. Kemp Clark, the senior physician in the trauma room when Kennedy died, told the Warren Commission that he "examined the wound in the back of the president's head. This was a large, gaping wound in the right posterior part, with cerebral and cerebellar tissue being damaged and exposed."

Dr. Robert McClelland, a surgeon, told the Warren Commission that he "could very closely examine the head wound, and...noted that the right posterior portion of the skull had been extremely blasted....you could actually look down into the skull cavity itself and see that probably a third or so, at least, of the brain tissue...had been blasted out."

These observations are significant for two reasons. First, entrance and exit wounds have a different character. As mentioned, a bullet almost always creates a small, neat sucking wound on entry because the bullet strikes nose on, punching in tissue.

But there is usually a larger and more torn, gaping wound on exit because the bullet often tumbles when passing through the body, dragging tissue behind it. So if the larger wound was in the back of the president's head, then that must have been the exit wound and the fatal shot must have come from the front.

Second, the trauma-room observations differ radically from those made that night by a second group of medical professionals—those at Bethesda Naval Hospital, near Washington.

Less than an hour after the president was declared dead, the Secret Service removed his body from Parkland Hospital. The Dallas County Medical Examiner, Earl Rose, tried to block the doorway, resisting its removal until an autopsy was performed. (And, legally, he was quite right to do so—in 1963, it was not a federal crime to murder a president, and so the federal authorities had no right to make off with the evidence.) But the Secret Service simply shifted him out of the way and left for Love Field.

From there the body was flown to Andrews Air Force Base near Washington, then driven to Bethesda Naval Hospital where an autopsy was finally performed on the president's corpse. There's disagreement about when the autopsy actually began; it was either six hours and forty-five minutes or nine hours after it left Dallas in Air Force One.

There are several mysteries shrouding the body during that time. According to Aubrey Rike, who helped prepare the body in Dallas, it was wrapped from head to toe in a sheet, then placed in a stately casket of ornamental bronze with white satin lining.

Yet according to Paul O'Connor, who assisted at Bethesda, it arrived at the autopsy zipped up in a grey rubber body bag inside what looked more like a "cheap shipping casket." Only the president's head was wrapped in a sheet.

There is also about an hour between the time the ambulance bearing the president and Mrs. Kennedy pulled up in front of Bethesda Naval Hospital and final delivery of the body through the back door to the autopsy room—an hour during which it seems to have disappeared.

Whatever happened to the president's corpse en route, the pathologists finally got to work under Commanders Hume and Boswell. Neither was an experienced forensic pathologist. This may explain why a routine procedure like tracing the bullets' tracks through the body does not appear to have been carried out.

But it does not explain why the wounds identified by the Washington personnel were so different from those of their Dallas colleagues. Where Parkland personnel saw a wound of front entry in the neck, Bethesda personnel saw an exit wound. Where Parkland was convinced that there was a massive wound of exit in the right rear of the president's head, Bethesda was equally convinced that the shot to the head hit from the rear and exited from the right-front temple area.

Bethesda x-rays show the whole right front area of the president's skull blasted away, including the right eye socket. And yet the autopsy photos show very clearly that the president's face and right temple area were intact. (See the facing page.)

Investigating these and other discrepancies in his book *Best Evidence*, David S. Lifton speculates that the president's wounds were altered surgically before the Bethesda autopsy began.

The acoustics evidence

Further support for a shot fired from the front came from a recording made by a policeman on a motorcycle in the motorcade several cars back from the president, who unwittingly got his microphone switch stuck in the "on" position. Through the microphone, the sounds of the Dealey Plaza gunfire were transmitted to police headquarters and automatically recorded on a low-fidelity Dictabelt system.

For years, a tape recording of this Dictabelt had been in the possession of Mary Ferrell of Dallas, the unofficial archivist for anti-Warren critics. Many had listened to it, but the quality was so poor and there were so many random bursts of static on it that it seemed uninterpretable.

In 1978, Ferrell brought this tape to the House Assassinations Committee, hoping it might surrender its secrets to high-tech analysis. The committee agreed to try, selecting an acoustics engineering and research laboratory at Bolt, Baranek and Newman (BBN) of Cambridge, Massachusetts to carry out the analysis.

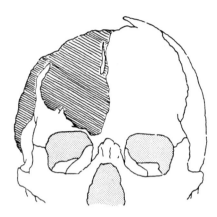

The tracing above is of an X-ray supposedly made of JFK's skull at Bethesda Naval Hospital. Note that the front right quadrant (to the left as you look at the picture) is missing.

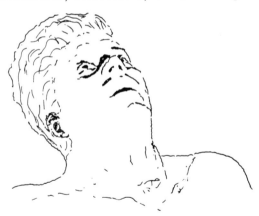

This second tracing is of an autopsy photo of JFK's corpse, also made at Bethesda. Note that the front right quadrant is intact. No one has yet explained this discrepancy. (The actual photos are in Lifton, <u>Best Evidence</u>.)

The first report from BBN was that the Ferrell copy could not be read: the quality was too poor. Then committee investigators found that another, better copy was in storage in the Dallas Police Department. A second report brought explosive news: BBN had detected four shots. Since the Warren Commission's theory held that the Depository sniper could only have fired three times, a second gunman had to be involved.

This finding was too important not to be challenged. The committee engaged two other expert acoustics engineers, Mark Weiss and Ernest Aschkenasy of the City University of New York, who analyzed echo patterns (an entirely different technique than that used by BBN) on BBN's cleaned-up tape. They confirmed BBN's findings and recommended that, to arrive at a definitive finding, the committee conduct live-ammunition tests in Dealey Plaza to see if the echo patterns they discerned on the tape could be duplicated.

The Dealey Plaza tests not only confirmed the finding of four shots but showed with 95% certainty that one of shots—the third—was fired from the grassy knoll. Further, the tape established a precise time between the first two shots: 1.6 seconds—a period too brief for Oswald's Mannlicher-Carcano.

The results were a masterpiece of scientific detection. The Justice Department, however, reacted with numb disbelief. At first it did nothing; then, later that year, gave the committee's findings to a panel selected by the National Academy of Sciences (NAS) to reevaluate the results.

While the scientific experts dithered, a nontechnical follower of the case named Steve Barber entered the picture. During the summer of 1979, he bought an issue of *Gallery*, a men's magazine, that contained a story on the Assassinations Committee's findings and had a 45-rpm disk of the acoustics tape bound into it.

Barber played this disk on a good stereo system and noticed that, just at the moment of the four shots, there was a faint voice signal. Listening more closely, he realized the voice was from a police transmission well known to have taken place about a minute after the shooting. The signal, in fact, referred to the shooting and therefore could not possibly have been simultaneous with it.

Barber came forward with his discovery and the NAS panel lapped it up, not bothering to conduct any technical tests of their own. Here was proof, the NAS reasoned, that the impulses BBN claimed were shots, and that were further analyzed by Weiss and Aschkenazy, could not have been shots at all.

The BBN scientists did not concede the point. Dr. James Barger, chief acoustical scientist for BBN, told British author Anthony Summers that the Dictabelt stylus might have jumped back after recording the shots, thus recording the voice message over the shots and creating an illusion that the two signals came in at the same time.

Dr. Barger further argued that the impulses identified as shots were precisely identified as such—not only the muzzle blast but the missile shock waves were identifiable on the tape. "The number of detections we made in our tests," Dr. Barger said, "and the speed of the detections—the odds that that could happen by chance are about one in twenty."

Evidence of another gunman

Taken together, the evidence that the fatal head shot was fired not from the Book Depository but from the grassy knoll is formidable:

- Numerous credible witnesses heard a shot from the front.

- Motorcycle policeman in the line of fire behind Kennedy were hit by bone and tissue.

- The Zapruder film showed what most viewers inter-pret as Kennedy's reaction to a front shot.

- Emergency room professionals in Dallas testified that, without a doubt, there was a massive exit wound in the back of Kennedy's head.

- The acoustics evidence identified four shots, one coming from in front of the president.

- There is no way a single gunman, using the alleged murder rifle, could possibly account for all the wounds and the time intervals between them.

The three tramps

If there was another gunman, who was it? There are several suspects among those arrested by the police that day in Dealey Plaza.

Union Pacific Railroad dispatcher Lee Bowers saw "between 50 and 100 policemen" come up the incline north of Elm "within a maximum of five minutes" and "seal off the area" around his railroad tower. Bowers told the Warren Commission that he "held off the trains until they could be examined, and there was [sic] some transients taken on at least one train."

These "transients" were three middle-aged men who have passed down into the literature of the assassination as "the three tramps." Photographs of them marching through Dealey Plaza with their captors reveal none of the usual signs of indigence, however. Their clothing is a bit rumpled but neither soiled nor ill-fitting, their hair is freshly barbered, they are clean-shaven and they seem in fine physical shape.

The tramps were taken by two policemen to the Dallas County Sheriff's office for questioning. But the police did not take down their names, did not make any known record of their interrogation, and did not report them to the FBI. Instead, the three were promptly released, and the police claimed that they had nothing to do with the shooting.

Since then, the tramps have been the focus of sometimes intense controversy as various Warren critics have attempted to identify them. Some people, quite implausibly, have claimed that the two shorter tramps were actually the CIA's E. Howard Hunt and Frank Sturgis of Watergate fame.

More persuasively, Dallas-based researcher Gary Mack has suggested that the tallest tramp is underworld hitman Charles V. Harrelson. Harrelson was indicted in 1980 along with the brother of New Orleans Mafia boss Carlos Marcello for the 1979 assassination of federal judge John Wood of San Antonio, shot in an ambush by a high-powered rifle. Now serving a life sentence at Texarkana Prison, Harrelson confessed in 1980 to the Wood killing and at the same time claimed a role in the JFK assassination.

In a prison interview in 1981, Dallas TV newsman Quin Mathews reminded Harrelson of his statement about the JFK assassination. Harrelson replied, "Well, do you believe Lee Harvey Oswald killed President Kennedy alone, without any aid from a rogue agency of the US Government or at least a portion of that agency? I believe you are very naive if you do." In a 1988 interview with a British TV investigator, Harrelson denied being the tall tramp but conceded that the resemblance to himself was striking.

Late in 1991, researcher Lois Gibson supported identification of Harrelson as the tallest tramp and produced a man named Chauncey Holt who claims to be one of the others. Holt says he was a career forger for the CIA and that his CIA boss, whom he named, directed his movements in Dallas during JFK's trip.

Other people in the area

Another man was photographed in the custody of a Dallas policeman in Dealey Plaza. Older, gray-haired, in a jacket and tie, he could not be described as a tramp. But his jacket is strangely long with what appears to be a straight, stiff object hidden underneath. As with the tramps, however, there is no mention of him in police records.

Several researchers have noted that the age, weight, height and build of this man exactly fit the FBI description of Joseph A. Milteer, a wealthy and militant right-wing extremist. Milteer is suspected of a role in the September 1963 bombing of a church in Birmingham, Alabama, in which four black children were killed. On November 9, 1963, Milteer discussed Kennedy's scheduled November 18 visit to Miami with a police informant there, who secretly taped the conversation:

Informant: Well, he will have a thousand bodyguards, don't worry about that.

Milteer: The more bodyguards he has, the easier it is to get him.

Informant: Well, how in the hell do you figure would be the best way to get him?

Milteer: From an office building with a high-powered rifle....He knows he's a marked man....

Informant: They are really going to try to kill him?

Milteer: Oh yeah, it is in the working....They will pick somebody up within hours afterward, if anything like that would happen. Just to throw the public off.

This threat was taken very seriously by the chief of Miami's Police Intelligence Bureau, Captain Charles Sapp. Seven months earlier, Sapp had warned the FBI and Secret Service that the Administration's order banning anti-Castro raids on Cuba had provoked a backlash: "The Cuban people feel that the US Government has turned against them....Violence hitherto directed toward Castro's Cuba will now be directed toward various governmental agencies in the United States."

A handbill appearing soon after in Miami invoked "an inspired Act of God" that would "place in the White House within weeks a Texan known to be a friend of all Latin Americans."

Although not photographed by bystanders, Jim Braden, a.k.a. Eugene Hale Brading, was also detained momentarily on the 22nd by Dallas police. Braden, a known Mafia courier with a record of thirty arrests, told police he was in Dallas on oil business. He was staying at the Cabana Hotel which Jack Ruby visited several days before the assassination.

More interesting yet was the arrest of Jack Lawrence who, on faked New Orleans references, got a job as a car salesman in October 1963 at Downtown Lincoln-Mercury, two blocks away from Dealey Plaza. The day before the assassination he borrowed a company car. The next morning he did not show up for work.

But half an hour after the assassination he appeared in the showroom pale, sweating and with mud on his clothes. He then hurried to the restroom and vomited. He told his co-workers he had been trying to return the car to work, had gotten stuck in traffic and had parked the car nearby.

Two co-workers went to retrieve it and found it parked behind the wooden fence just north of Dealey Plaza, overlooking the grassy knoll. Lawrence's behavior aroused the suspicions of another co-worker, who called the police. Lawrence was held overnight, then released.

The ghost on the grassy knoll

Even though we have ample evidence that there was a second gunman, that he was shooting from the grassy knoll area in front of the president and in fact fired the fatal shot to JFK's head, that gunman's identity remains a mystery. There is, however, a piece of evidence that comes tantalizingly close to identifying that gunman.

Phillip Willis was standing on the south side of Elm Street directly across from the Book Depository. Just after the first shot rang out, Willis took a color picture catching the grassy knoll just behind the presidential limo. The knoll is blurred and out of focus, but independent analysts have long claimed to discern a ghostly figure there in exactly the spot from which the acoustics evidence was to reveal a shot was fired.

The Warren Commission did not examine this photograph, but the Assassinations Committee gave it to the Aerospace Corporation, which used computer-assisted means to enhance the image. "This computer display" reported the committee, "made visible an object whose size and shape were consistent with a human being, positioned just inside the retaining wall..., most probably an adult person...." There was even blurred evidence of a firearm: "near the region of the hands is a very distinct straight-line feature extending from lower right to upper left."

A second photograph, taken by Mary Moorman, also suggests a ghostly figure on the knoll. It is less clear than Willis's but, even so, analysts Gary Mack and Jack White claim they see a figure in the picture, wearing what might be a police uniform and firing a weapon. This figure has become known as "badge man" because there appears to be a badge on his chest.

Although the photographic analysis in neither case is conclusive, new techniques may one day reveal more of the photographs' secrets.

Was Oswald involved?

Even if we can't identify the second gunman, can we be sure that Oswald was the first? If he had stood trial, would there have been sufficient evidence to convict?

Although there is some physical evidence linking Oswald with the Dealey Plaza shooting—he was in the Book Depository on November 22 and owned the rifle found in the sixth floor sniper's nest from which the "magic bullet" was shot—a strong case can be made in his defense.

First, his actions immediately before and after the shooting were hardly those of an assassin. He was seen in a relaxed mood having lunch in the Depository lunchroom as late as 12:15 by Carolyn Arnold, secretary to the Depository's vice president. Had the presidential motorcade not been running late, it would have been only ten minutes away from Dealey Plaza, leaving Oswald little time to prepare for the shooting.

As it was, the motorcade turned into Dealey Plaza at 12:30. Within two minutes of the shooting—

during which time Oswald would have just run down four flights of stairs, according to the Warren Commission—police officer Marrion Baker encountered Oswald "standing in the lunchroom drinking a Coke."

Building supervisor Roy Truly, accompanying Baker, observed that Oswald "didn't seem to be excited or overly afraid." Another Depository employee saw Oswald seconds after this and noted "he was very calm."

Second, in tests conducted by crack shots, the feat of marksmanship attributed to Oswald was never duplicated. The Warren Commission claimed that Oswald, rated a poor shot in the Marines, hit a moving target with two out of three shots at a range of almost a hundred yards, and did so while firing through a misaligned sight at a virtually impossible rate of fire.

Not even with stationary targets have the finest professional marksmen been able to equal this achievement. It was only by adopting the farcical assumption that Oswald merely point-aimed his weapon (that is, used neither the telescopic scope nor the "iron sights" on top of the scope but simply fired in the general direction of the target) that the experts could even fire the required number of shots within the time limits imposed by the Zapruder film.

Third, crime-lab examination of the Mannlicher-Carcano rifle could not identify a single finger or palm print on it as Oswald's. Several days after the event, the Dallas police reported finding a bit of Oswald's palm print on a part of the barrel that is exposed only when the rifle is disassembled. But not even the Warren Commission, hungry as it was for evidence to incriminate Oswald, found this convincing.

As an FBI memo of August 28, 1964, noted: "There was a serious question in the minds of the commission as to whether or not the palm print impression...from the Dallas Police Department is a legitimate latent palm impression removed from the rifle barrel or whether it was obtained from some other source...." A Dallas police expert testified to the commission that he "could not make a positive identification of these prints."

Fourth, the nitrate tests given Oswald to determine if he had shot a firearm were negative for his cheeks, indicating that he had not fired a rifle. The nitrates found on his hands were consistent with firing a handgun, but they also could have been deposited by handling a newspaper or boxes.

Fifth, Oswald's wife Marina testified to the FBI that "Oswald didn't have any ammunition for the rifle to her knowledge in either Dallas or New Orleans, and he didn't speak of buying ammunition." The FBI checked Dallas gun shops and interviewed salesmen, but were unable to find evidence that ammunition was sold either to Oswald or someone named Alek Hidell.

Sixth, the "magic bullet" discovered at Parkland Hospital and determined to have been fired from Oswald's gun may have been planted. Not only is the bullet too pristine to have traveled through both JFK and Connally, but it may never have fallen from Connally's body at all.

When Darrell Tomlinson turned the bullet over to Secret Service agent Richard Johnson, Tomlinson reported that it rolled off a stretcher—but not the one used by Connally. Tomlinson later changed his story to say that the bullet had, in fact, come from the Connally stretcher, but only after being repeatedly pressed by the Warren Commission to do so.

The suspicion that "the magic bullet" was planted becomes even stronger when we consider a second bullet that rolled out of JFK's casket when it was opened at Bethesda Naval Hospital. Chief of Surgery David P. Osborne picked it up, noting that it "was not deformed in any way." This second bullet was turned over to the FBI, which acknowledged its receipt in writing. But it then disappeared.

Seventh, the photos the Warren Commission used to establish that Oswald owned both murder weapons—not only the Mannlicher-Carcano rifle but also the .38 special Smith & Wesson revolver he allegedly used to kill Tippit—may show signs of forgery, as Oswald himself claimed when he first saw them. (Take a look at them on the next page and judge for yourself.)

There is an awkward, off-balance relationship between the figure and background: although the body is larger in one photo, the head seems exactly the same size in each, and the shadow of Oswald's nose on his face points in a different direction than the shadow of his body on the ground.

Oswald immediately asserted that the figure in the photo had his face but not his body and that, as Dallas police captain Will Fritz paraphrased him, he

These photographs are supposed to show Oswald in his back yard holding a rifle and left-wing literature. When Oswald saw them, he immediately said that his head had been pasted onto someone else's body. Note that, in both pictures, the shadow of the nose points straight down but the shadow of the body angles to the left.

"would be able to show that it was not his picture and that it had been made by someone else."

This was precisely the view of these photos that Mark Lane and other critics had been voicing for six months before Oswald's claim was published in the Warren Report. Scotland Yard and Canadian Defense Department intelligence experts also later agreed that the photos were forgeries.

Oswald and General Walker

All too aware, perhaps, that the physical evidence linking Oswald to the JFK assassination was scant, the Warren Commission looked beyond Dealey Plaza to two other shootings—that of Dallas patrolman J.D. Tippit the same day, and of Major General Edwin Walker seven months earlier—to construct a psychological portrait of Oswald as a violent assassin.

General Walker, a Korean War hero, angrily resigned from the US Army in 1961 after JFK had reprimanded him for political indoctrination of the troops. Returning home to Dallas, Walker ran for governor on an extreme right-wing platform and, in 1962, led a mob to oppose JFK's order to desegregate the University of Mississippi.

On April 10, 1963, a shot was fired at Walker through a window in his home. It missed him and buried itself in a wall. Police investigating the case failed to turn up any significant leads—until Oswald was taken into custody on November 22 and Walker's name and phone number were discovered in his address book.

Marina Oswald later told the Warren Commission that her husband came home late on April 10 "very pale," saying that "he had shot at General Walker," run "several kilometers" and "buried the rifle" in a field by a railroad track before taking the bus home. Oswald then showed Marina five photos of Walker's house.

The Warren Commission seized upon Marina's testimony not only to declare Oswald guilty of the attempted Walker shooting but to further substantiate his guilt in the JFK assassination. Although the commission noted that it "could not make any definitive determination of Oswald's motives" in either shooting, the Walker incident "demonstrated [Oswald's] disposition to take human life....and his capacity for violence..."

The commission further theorized that, since Oswald left a note for Marina (which was undated but found by her on the evening of April 10) requesting that she collect news stories about him if anything should happen, his motive was to make a name for himself—"an important factor to consider in assessing possible motivation for the [JFK] assassination." But in their haste to link the Walker incident with the JFK assassination, the commission ignored other pertinent facts of the case.

First, Oswald's alleged "capacity for violence" does not explain why he would kill two men as politically diverse as JFK and Walker. Marina testified that Oswald praised JFK but called Walker a "fascist," "compared [him] to Adolf Hitler" and remarked that "if someone had killed Hitler in time it would have saved many lives."

Second, there was no material evidence connecting Oswald to the Walker incident. The bullet discovered in Walker's house was identified by the police to the press as a 30.06-caliber bullet and in their report as "steel-jacketed, of unknown caliber"—not a 6.5-mm copper-jacketed bullet like the ones supposedly shot from Oswald's rifle in Dealey Plaza.

Experts Robert A. Frazier and Joseph D. Nicol both reported that the Walker bullet "could have been fired from [Oswald's] rifle," but because of its deformed condition "could not be identified as having been fired or not fired from that rifle."

Third, none of the men seen near Walker's before or at the time of the shooting looked like Oswald. In early April, a Walker aide saw two men prowling outside his employer's home and a "Cuban or dark-complected man in a 1957 Chevrolet" who circled the house several times.

Immediately after the shooting, 15-year-old Walter Coleman, who had been standing in a nearby doorway, went to look over the fence into the alley and brightly lit church lot behind Walker's house. Questioned by the FBI after Dealey Plaza but never called by the Warren Commission, Coleman reported seeing two white men—neither resembling Oswald—getting into separate cars, a 1950 Ford and a 1958 Chevrolet. Oswald did not know how to drive.

Fourth, the Warren Commission ignored the fact that someone tampered with the Walker evidence after Oswald's death. In a copy (published by the commission) of one of the photographs Oswald took of the Walker house, the license plate of a 1957

Chevrolet parked behind the house was cut out, yet in Oswald's original the license plate was intact—although too small and unclear for the numbers to be read.

Oswald and Officer Tippet

The evidence incriminating Oswald in the murder of J.D. Tippitt is even more dubious. According to the Warren Commission, Oswald fled Dealey Plaza after the JFK shooting and headed for his rooming house, where he picked up his pistol. It was after he left his room that he was spotted by Patrolman Tippit, alone in his squad car. The commission said that Tippit pulled his car to the curb and got out to approach Oswald on foot, and that when he reached the left front of the car, Oswald fired, hitting him four times and killing him instantly.

But in order to reach the Tippit murder scene by 1:16 pm—the latest, according to the police, the murder could have been committed— Oswald must have traveled faster than the "brisk walk" speed of four miles an hour from his room almost a mile away. If the murder was in fact committed minutes earlier, as three witnesses claimed it was, it would have been nearly impossible for Oswald to reach the murder scene. None of the witnesses reported seeing a man running.

Moreover, the eyewitness testimony was confusing and contradictory. Of the sixteen eyewitnesses to some aspect of the Tippit shooting, only one, Helen Markham, actually identified Oswald, and Markham was an unreliable witness. Warren

Commission Senior Counsel Joseph Ball called her an "utter screwball" and Wesley Liebeler, another Warren Commission attorney, deemed her testimony "worthless."

Domingo Benavides, who was sitting in his truck across the street and thus closest to the Tippit murder, could not identify Oswald. Of the six Tippit eyewitnesses who identified Oswald as the man leaving the scene of the shooting, five did so at a police lineup where Oswald, his face bruised and swollen, protested loudly that he had been framed and identified himself as a worker at the Texas School Book Depository, the site already well known as the assassin's lair.

The sixth of these witnesses, Warren Reynolds, initially told the FBI that he could not positively identify Oswald. He changed his mind after recovering from a shot in the head fired by an unknown assailant two days later.

Three eyewitnesses whom the Warren Commission decided not to interview said that Tippit was confronted by two men rather than one, that the one who did not shoot fled the scene in an automobile and that, unlike Oswald, the assailant had a chunky build and black, bushy hair.

The ballistics evidence was also ambiguous. The four bullets in Tippit's body and the four spent casings found on the scene support testimony that Tippit's killer ejected spent shells as he fled. But the type of bullets in the body did not match the casings. Three of the bullets were Western-Winchesters; the last was a Remington-Peters. Yet two of the casings were made by Western-Winchester, the other two by Remington-Peters.

To explain this, the Warren Commission and later the House Assassinations Committee decided that Oswald must have fired a Remington round somewhere else before he shot Tippit, but just had not ejected the shell, and that the shell from the second Western bullet found in Tippit's body simply went undiscovered.

There are other anomalies. First, the policeman who collected the casings at the scene marked them with his initials, as is standard procedure. But when the casings were examined later by the Warren Commission, they were without markings.

Second, at the scene of the murder the casings were expertly identified from their ejection markings as having been fired from an automatic; Oswald's pistol was a revolver. Third, the Dallas police turned over only one bullet to the FBI at first. It was not until March 1964 that they gave them the other three. The FBI could identify none of these four bullets as having been fired from Oswald's revolver.

Oswald, the FBI and the CIA

The commission's political portrait of Oswald was even more incriminating than the psychological one, emphasizing his alleged communist sympathies and presenting him as confused but decidedly left-wing.

During his last month in the Marines, Oswald applied for a hardship discharge for no good reason (citing a minor and already-healed injury to his mother's hand). He then defected to the Soviet Union and declared himself a Communist.

He recanted after a year and half and returned to the United States with his Russian wife, Marina—only to once again announce himself a member of the Communist Party and become the founding and only member of the New Orleans chapter of the Fair Play for Cuba Committee. He passed out pro-Castro leaflets twice in New Orleans.

In the fall of 1963, he (or someone calling himself Oswald) traveled to Mexico City and visited both the Cuban consulate and the Soviet embassy, apparently hoping to obtain travel visas to Cuba and the Soviet Union.

When the House Assassinations Committee investigated Oswald, it discovered that the Warren Commission had overlooked or ignored a more complex political past. In 1960, Oswald was assigned to the top-secret U-2 spy plane base in Japan and received Russian-language training and instruction in Marxism-Leninism, as though being prepared for intelligence work. Indeed, a Navy intelligence operative named Gerry Hemming stated that Oswald was "some type of agent" in 1959.

One of the few memos released from Oswald's massive CIA file also indicated that the agency considered recruiting him while in Russia: "We were particularly interested in the [information] Oswald might provide on the Minsk factory in which he had been employed [and] on certain sections of the city itself."

And in the summer of 1963, Oswald spent time in New Orleans with both Guy Banister, a former FBI officer and leading figure in militant anti-Castro Cuban exile groups, and David Ferrie, a former contract agent for the CIA in raids against Cuba.

While pursuing the question of who Oswald really was, the House Committee found even more extraordinary evidence: the CIA transcriptions and photographs used to document Oswald's Mexico City trip—a key piece of the Warren Commission portrait—indicated that someone else had used Oswald's name.

Transcriptions of taped conversations between "Oswald" and Soviet embassy officials indicated he spoke garbled Russian—yet the real Oswald's Russian was fluent. Photographs of the Oswald who visited the Cuban consulate and Soviet embassy showed a large, powerfully-built man in his mid-30s, described in the CIA teletype as an "American...approximately 35 years old, with an athletic build, about six feet tall [and] receding hairline." (See the photograph on the next page.) Oswald was 24, about 5' 9" and slender.

But having discovered this impressive new evidence, the House committee chose not to pursue the obvious implications—that Oswald did have ties, however ambiguous, to US intelligence, that his leftist activities may have been part of his cover as an agent and that he may have been impersonated in Mexico City. Instead, the committee endorsed the Warren Commission's portrait of Oswald.

The CIA said that the man in this photograph, which was taken shortly before the assassination outside either the Soviet or Cuban embassy in Mexico City (which were both monitored 24 hours a day) was Lee Harvey Oswald. It was immediately obvious that he bears no physical resemblance to Oswald. The CIA could never produce any pictures at all of Oswald in Mexico City.

The CIA called the Mexico City data a "mix-up" (without explaining how the mix-up happened) and the House Committee accepted this explanation. Strangely, however, it classified its lengthy report on Oswald's Mexican trip and sequestered it until the year 2029.

It is only from a 1988 TV interview that we have some inkling of what the committee found. An investigator for the House Committee, Juan Edwin Lopez, at risk of violating his oath of secrecy but clearly frustrated by it, stated that the committee believed Oswald had gone to Mexico City but not to the Soviet embassy or Cuban consulate, and that "the only plausible explanation [for the implied Oswald impersonation] is that they [CIA agents, rogue or otherwise] were trying to set [Oswald] up."

If Lopez's statement is accurate, it supports other fragmentary evidence of an Oswald set-up. For example, in the three years preceding Dealey Plaza at least six other Oswald impersonations had taken place:

- An FBI memo dated January 3, 1960, noted that "there's a possibility that an imposter is using Oswald's birth certificate."

- On January 20, 1961, "Oswald" and a powerfully-built Latin man visited the Bolton Ford dealership in New Orleans, looking for a deal on ten pick-up trucks needed by the Friends of Democratic Cuba. On this date, Oswald was in the Soviet Union.

- On September 25, 1963, a man calling himself Oswald requested that the Selective Service Office in

Austin help him upgrade his discharge from undesirable. On this date, Oswald was supposedly in transit to Mexico City.

- In October of that year, a highly credible Cuban exile, Sylvia Odio, and her sister were visited in Dallas by "Oswald" and two other men recruiting support for the anti-Castro cause. On this date the Warren Commission placed Oswald either in New Orleans or en route to Mexico.

- On November 1, a man later identified by three witnesses as Oswald entered a gun shop in Fort Worth to buy ammunition. The Warren Commission had evidence that Oswald was at work that day in Dallas.

- On November 9, a man calling himself Oswald walked into a Lincoln-Mercury showroom in Dallas and asked to take a car for a test spin. The salesman found the ride unforgettable—"Oswald" reached speeds of 85 mph while delivering a harangue about capitalist credit and the superiority of the Soviet system. The real Oswald did not know how to drive a car, and the Warren Commission placed him at home in Irving, Texas, on that day.

Then there were several peculiarities suggesting complicity on the day of the assassination itself. First, bystander Charles L. Bronson, standing at the intersection of Main and Houston, caught the sixth-floor window of the Texas Book Depository with his 8mm movie camera just as the presidential motorcade was passing by.

The images are blurred, but at least one of the House Committee's photo analysts believes that three figures can be identified in the sniper's nest. The committee got Bronson's film too late for thorough analysis but recommended that "because of its high quality, it...be analyzed further."

Second, Deputy Sheriff Roger Craig, who saw Oswald at the police station after the assassination, was "positive that Oswald is identical with the same individual he observed...run down the grass area from the direction of the Texas School Book Depository..., whistle" and get into a white Rambler station wagon that pulled up to the curb—all within a few minutes of the shooting. The Warren Commission disregarded this testimony since it conflicted with the official reconstruction of Oswald's activities.

Third, Oswald's description was broadcast on the police radio within fifteen minutes of the shooting. According to Warren Commission attorney Wesley Leibeler, this fact should have been a red flag to the commission because it implied "that Oswald had been picked out as a patsy before the event."

And fourth, shortly after Oswald arrived at his rooming house at 1 pm that same day, his housekeeper, Earlene Roberts, noticed a squad car with two uniformed policemen in it pull up outside. The driver tapped the horn twice, then drove slowly away. Within minutes, Oswald emerged from his room and left.

Would Oswald have been convicted had he stood trial? Since much of the evidence is still secret, we can not know for sure. But the evidence we do have suggests that there is at least reasonable doubt of his guilt. He may only have been, as he said, "the patsy."

Ruby's ties to the Mafia

Jack Ruby gunned down Lee Oswald less than 48 hours after the Kennedy assassination, claiming he acted on impulse and out of "shock and grief" at JFK's death. The Warren Commission accepted this explanation despite significant findings to the contrary.

First, there was evidence that the murder was planned in advance. Early in the morning of November 24, the Dallas FBI and County Sheriff's office received anonymous phone tips that Oswald was marked for assassination. A dispatcher who took one of the calls knew Ruby and said he was the caller.

Second, when Ruby insisted on being interviewed by the commission in June 1964, he strongly suggested that his original story was untrue. As he told Earl Warren and Gerald Ford (who had been reluctant to interview him), "Since I have a spotty background in the nightclub business, I should have been the last person to even want to do [it]."

In other words, Ruby was trying to tell the commissioners that his career, which put him in touch with the Dallas underworld, should alert them to the implausibility of his story. Why would he, of all people, be driven to murder out of grief for JFK?

Then Ruby went on, as if imploring the commissioners to dig deeper, yet fearful of saying too much. He said that he had "been used for a purpose, and [that] there will be a certain tragic occurrence happening if you don't take my testimony and somehow vindicate me." But Warren and Ford were not interested in deciphering Ruby's cryptic remarks.

Instead, they reaffirmed the commission's earlier conclusion that Ruby was yet another lone nut.

When the House Assassinations Committee investigated Ruby, it uncovered evidence that he was not a lone nut at all but had extensive links to organized crime. As a teenager in Chicago, Ruby was a runner for Al Capone, and later a labor racketeer.

He moved to Dallas in 1947 and became point man for mob relations with the police. He made several trips to Cuba for the Mafia, possibly to ransom Florida Mafioso Santos Trafficante from a Cuban prison. He was in telephone contact with at least 29 Mafia personalities in the months preceding Dealey Plaza.

Given his history, the committee concluded that it would have been entirely out of character for Ruby to kill Oswald on impulse and that he was probably ordered to do so. It further suspected, but was unable to establish with certainty, that Ruby was aided by others; given the tight security at the city jail, it seemed unlikely "that Ruby entered the police basement [where the murder took place] without assistance...."

The committee never did find out from Ruby what assistance he might have had; he died of cancer in Parkland Hospital on January 3, 1967. But shortly before dying, Ruby spoke approvingly of a book that was critical of the Warren Commission's version and that suggested that a conspiracy had taken place: Thomas G. Buchanan's *Who Killed Kennedy?*

Dead witnesses

Investigations have been thwarted by the number of material witnesses who died in the first few years after the assassination and in periods of renewed interest in the case during the 1970s. Researcher Jim Marrs counts a total of 94 "convenient" deaths through 1979, when the House Committee ended its work, of which Marrs labels 60 "particularly suspicious." Thirteen occurred in the three years following Dealey Plaza.

While Marrs may overdraw the sinister implications of these deaths, many key witnesses have indeed died at strategically important moments. Here are a few of the more interesting cases:

- Gary Underhill, a CIA agent who claimed the CIA was involved in the JFK assassination, died of a gunshot to the head in May 1964. His death was ruled a suicide.

- Guy Banister, a former FBI agent and acquaintance of Oswald, died of an apparent heart attack in June 1964. Files containing information on his anti-Castro activities were missing by the time authorities reached his office.

- Mary Meyer, a mistress of JFK's during the White House years and the estranged wife of CIA veteran Cord Meyer, was murdered in October 1964 in a park in Washington, DC. Cord Meyer was a fishing companion of CIA counter-intelligence chief, James Jesus Angleton, who seized Meyer's diary after her death.

- C.D. Jackson, senior vice president of *Life* magazine, died of unknown causes in September 1964. Jackson arranged for *Life* to buy the Zapruder film soon after the Dealey Plaza shooting and then locked it away. (The film was not widely seen by the public until it was shown on ABC's *Goodnight America* in 1975.)

- Rose Cheramie, a prostitute and striptease dancer in Ruby's Dallas nightclub, died in a Texas hit-and-run accident in September 1965. Two days before the assassination, she told police in Louisiana she overheard two Latin men plotting to kill the president.

- Dorothy Kilgallen, a prominent columnist and TV personality, was ruled a suicide by drug overdose in November 1965. She had just completed a lengthy interview of Ruby in prison and told friends privately that she was about to "break" the JFK case.

- David Ferrie, a militant anti-Castroite and associate of Oswald and Banister, died of an apparent brain embolism in February 1967. He was just about to be arraigned for conspiracy in the JFK assassination by New Orleans District Attorney Jim Garrison, whose investigation convinced him that the CIA was involved.

- Eladio Del Valle, a friend and political comrade of Ferrie's, was shot at close range the day after Ferrie's death. Garrison had been trying to find Del Valle for questioning.

- Hale Boggs, House majority leader and a member of the Warren Commission, was killed in a plane crash in Alaska in 1972. He had begun to express public doubts about the Warren Commission's findings.

- J.A. Milteer, the far-right Miami activist, died when his heater exploded in February 1974. As mentioned above, he predicted an attempt on JFK's life and the capture of a scapegoat shortly before events in Dealey Plaza—and a man looking a lot like him was picked up by the police that November afternoon.

- Clay Shaw, whom Garrison brought to trial as a prime suspect in a JFK conspiracy, died of cancer in August 1974. Unable to prove Shaw's CIA connections, Garrison saw him acquitted in 1969. But just a year after Shaw's death, a high-level CIA defector, Victor Marchetti, confirmed Shaw's ties to the agency.

- Sam Giancana, Mafia boss of Chicago, was shot to death in the basement of his home while in the Federal Witness Protection Program in June 1975. At the time of his murder, Giancana was scheduled to testify to the Senate Intelligence Committee on the CIA's alliance with the Mafia in an attempt to kill Castro.

- John Roselli, a Mafia lieutenant of Giancana's, was dismembered, stuffed into an oil drum and dropped into the ocean off Miami in July 1976. Roselli was the Mafia's contact man for its assassination projects with the CIA and was scheduled for a second appearance before the Senate Intelligence Committee when he was killed.

- George de Mohrenschildt, who befriended Oswald in Dallas, was found dead of a gunshot wound, deemed self-inflicted, in March 1977. Two hours before his death, an investigator for the House Assassinations Committee came to interview him about the JFK case, but de Mohrenschildt was not at home.

In a manuscript found afterwards, de Mohrenschildt supported Oswald's view of himself as "a patsy."

- Charles Nicoletti, also on the House Committee's witness list, was shot three times in the back of the neck in the parking lot of a suburban Chicago shopping center in March 1977—less than 48 hours after de Mohrenschildt's death. Nicoletti was said to have been a "handler" (that is, supervisor) of Mafia assassins in the CIA-Mafia plots.

- Carlos Prio Socarras, a president of pre-revolutionary Cuba, was found dying of a pistol shot in April 1977, just six days after Nicoletti was gunned down. Prio's death was ruled a suicide. He, too, was on the House Committee's witness list because of his alleged links to Jack Ruby and anti-Castro Cuban militants.

We may never know for sure if these key witnesses were murdered to keep them silent. But there is no doubt these deaths have significantly hindered the official investigations and the public's understanding of what took place at Dealey Plaza on November 22, 1963.

Evidence of a cover-up

The evidence that there was a cover-up is just as impressive as the evidence that there was a conspiracy in the first place. Here is a brief run-down, including a couple of points not mentioned above:

- Oswald's description was broadcast over police radio within fifteen minutes of the assassination. No one knows how this description was obtained.

- No interrogation records were kept for those arrested at Dealey Plaza, or for Oswald.

- The pictures of Oswald holding a gun appear to be faked.

- JFK's body was removed from Dallas before an autopsy could be performed there.

- JFK's corpse left Dallas wrapped in a sheet inside an ornamental bronze casket. It arrived at Bethesda Naval Hospital in Washington in a body bag inside a plain casket.

- The autopsy photographs of JFK's wounds differed radically from the descriptions of the doctors at Parkland Hospital.

- A whole tray of evidence, including what was left of the president's brain, remains missing from the National Archives.

- The pristine condition of "the magic bullet" suggests it was planted.

- Numerous films made by witnesses to the event were confiscated.

- Many more witnesses have died than would normally be expected, many in mysterious circumstances.

- Both the FBI and the CIA concealed important evidence from the Warren Commission.

- Critical data unearthed by the Warren Commission in 1964 and the Assassination Committee in 1978 is still classified secret.

Chapter Four

Who was involved?

I have reviewed a great deal of evidence that points away from the Warren Commission's lone-assassin theory, and that even suggests that Oswald never fired a gun. The magic bullet, alteration of the president's wounds, switching of the coffins and much else all point to a cover-up.

There certainly have been attempts to conceal the full story. Some Warren Commission evidence has been sequestered until 2039, some House Assassinations Committee material can not be viewed until 2029, and the Lopez report and CIA information on Oswald's alleged anti-Castro activities are classified as secret.

If there was a conspiracy to kill JFK, who was involved in it? Since secrecy pervades the case, and since so many witnesses have died, it is impossible to say with certainty, but the following six scenarios describe the most basic possibilities.

The Soviets

Two related theories propose that Nikita Khrushchev, humiliated by the 1962 Missile Crisis, instigated the assassination. One proposes that Oswald was directed to kill JFK by Valery Kostikov, a Mexico City Soviet embassy official and reputed KGB assassin overseer. The second proposes that the KGB captured Oswald during his stay in Russia and then sent an impersonator back to the US to kill the president.

An important advocate of the Kostikov theory was the CIA's chief of counter-intelligence operations, James Jesus Angleton. Either because he wanted to provoke a Soviet-American clash or because he really believed it, Angleton strenuously maintained that the KGB was behind the Kennedy assassination. In fact, the intensity of his conviction led to one of the most bizarre subplots in the entire JFK case and nearly destroyed the CIA from the inside out.

Early in 1964, a KGB officer named Yuri Nosenko, who had been informing to the CIA for more than a year, decided to defect and come to the United States. Nosenko had worked in the KGB bureau that kept the file on Oswald. He stated that he knew for a fact that Oswald was *not* under the control of the KGB.

But Angleton thought Nosenko was a "mole"—a fake defector whose real mission was to misinform the CIA. Angleton imprisoned Nosenko in a CIA safe house and pressured him in every way short of physical torture to deny what he had said. This situation led to a virtual war within the CIA, and ultimately resulted in Angleton's downfall and Nosenko's vindication.

The Soviets-did-it theory explains why the Warren Commission developed its implausible lone-assassin conclusion. According to Warren's *Memoirs*, Johnson had called him to the White House to tell him of "rumors floating around the world" that the Soviets might have been responsible, that if this were known "it might lead us into war," perhaps even a nuclear war, and that as many as 40 million people might die. Warren's *Memoirs* imply that the real job of the Warren Commission was to quiet any suspicion of Soviet guilt.

But the Soviet theory raises more questions than it answers. Why would the USSR risk nuclear war to promote LBJ, a much more militant Cold Warrior than JFK? Why would the Soviets trust Oswald? And how could Oswald's mother and brothers have been deceived by an Oswald double? (In 1981 Marina and Marguerite, Oswald's mother, were sufficiently persuaded by the theory to exhume Oswald's body. Dental records proved that the body buried in Oswald's grave was, in fact, Oswald's.)

Castro's Cuba

Another theory, popular among right-wingers and anti-Castroites (among them, US ambassador to Mexico Thomas Mann, columnist Jack Anderson and Mafia lieutenant John Roselli) accuses Fidel Castro of engineering the assassination. In this scenario, Castro either recruited Oswald as the assassin or turned around a hit squad that had been sent to kill him, sending them back to shoot JFK.

This theory has certain strengths. Like the Soviet theory, it suggests a motivation for the Warren Commission's cover-up—to protect the world from the consequences of learning about a Communist-directed assassination. Castro had a motive: The CIA had sponsored Mafia attempts against his life, and he had warned JFK that these attacks might "boomerang."

But this theory is also implausible. As Castro pointed out in a 1991 interview on NBC, Cuba had been improving its relations with JFK ever since the Missile Crisis and had nothing to gain by putting Johnson in the White House. Further, Cuba would have suffered extreme consequences if such a plot had been discovered.

Finally, if Oswald were the assassin, how was he recruited by Castro? Although Oswald had passed out pro-Castro leaflets in New Orleans, he did not associate with any other pro-Castro groups and had never visited Cuba.

The Mafia

In its final report of 1979, the House Assassinations Committee theorized that the assassination might have been masterminded by New Orleans Mafia boss Carlos Marcello. This view was endorsed by the committee's Chief Counsel, G. Robert Blakey, and Richard Billings in their 1981 book, *The Plot to Kill the President*, which suggests that two Mafia hitmen were involved—Oswald, firing from the book depository and another, still unknown, firing from the grassy knoll.

Marcello certainly had sufficient motive. Despite the Mafia's crucial help getting JFK elected in 1960, Marcello was apprehended and deported only a few months after JFK took office. Upon reentering the US and successfully contesting his deportation, Marcello threatened JFK's life and spoke of getting "a nut" to kill him.

Clearly the Mafia would not have used someone as inexperienced as Oswald as an assassin, so if he was involved, it must simply have been as a patsy.

And clearly the Mafia could not have done the job all by itself, since that would not explain the government cover-up. One possibility is that it blackmailed the government, demanding a cover-up in exchange for keeping secret the CIA's hiring of Mafia assassins to kill Castro. But more likely, it was simply hired to do the job.

A five-part TV series , *The Men Who Killed Kennedy*, which first aired in this country on the A&E cable network in the fall of 1991, provided testimony from two sources which sought to indicate that that three hitmen from the Corsican Mafia had been hired to do the job by the US Mafia.

New evidence emerged in 1991 that J. Edgar Hoover knew of a Mafia murder contract on JFK as early as September 1962 but never informed the Secret Service. According to Texas attorney Mark North, Hoover—a bitter foe of many of Kennedy's policies—was worried that Kennedy would enforce his mandatory retirement in 1965. North says that Hoover had earlier attempted to blackmail Kennedy with FBI evidence of his philandering, including JFK's sharing of a girlfriend with Mafia boss Sam Giancana.

The Cowboys

Another theory claims that JFK was assassinated by the Cowboys—wealthy and powerful Southwesterners who share national power in an uneasy balance with the more liberal East Coast political establishment, the Yankees. In this scenario, Oswald was manipulated into the role of patsy and was not an assassin.

The strong point of the Cowboy theory is that, as we have seen, many Texans were murderously angry at JFK by the summer of 1963. He had scaled back the oil depletion tax credit, disciplined General Edwin Walker and was, rumor had it, considering dumping another Texan, Lyndon Johnson, from his 1964 ticket.

There is at least one major weaknesses to this theory—if the Cowboys were planning to murder the president, why would they virtually advertise their intentions in advance?

The Mongoose team

The theory that seems most popular among researchers—Jim Garrison, Mark Lane, Fletcher Prouty, Robert Groden, David Lifton and Jim Marrs among them—is that the assassination was organized "off the reservation" by rogue agents associated with Operation Mongoose.

Mongoose was the code-name for programs JFK set up in the Defense Department, CIA and State Department after the Bay of Pigs to coordinate anti-Castro activities—some of which were aimed at overthrowing him by political and economic means, others at assassinating him outright. To carry out the JFK killing and to cover up their own involvement, Mongoose rogues set up Oswald, a low-level Naval intelligence agent, as a patsy and planted false clues pointing to Cuba, the Soviet Union and the Mafia.

This scenario also provides a clear motive for assassination. Mongoose members—particularly those in Task Force W, a CIA portion of the team—

were angry at JFK for his retreat from the Bay of Pigs and what they perceived as his concessions to Communism. As they saw it, LBJ's foreign policy would be a lot better.

This theory also explains how an official investigation could be thwarted and how Oswald, if he were a US intelligence operative in contact with Mongoose members, could have been framed. The difficulties lie not in the theory itself but in the impossibility of evaluating it without obtaining information now classified secret by the US government.

The Nazis

The most extreme theory traces the assassination to a group in the Defense Department that emerged around Werner von Braun and the Nazi rocket scientists the US military imported into the country, illegally and against specific orders, and installed at Huntsville, Alabama at the end of WWII—the famous Operation Paperclip.

During the same period, the US government also absorbed a network of Nazi spies headed by Nazi General Reinhard Gehlen. "The Gehlen Org" (as it came to be called) worked within the US government to promote Nazi aims and to protect and resettle Nazis from Europe. In fact, the CIA was built around the Gehlen Org.

This theory postulates an incredible degree of fascist corruption within the US intelligence services. But one person who lends it plausibility is Clay Shaw, the New Orleans businessman District Attorney Jim Garrison tried for conspiracy in 1968 (and failed to convict). An exit poll of the Shaw jury indicated that Garrison lost his case because he was unable to prove that Shaw was connected to the CIA.

But the year Shaw died (1974), a book by a highly placed CIA defector, Victor Marchetti, revealed that the CIA helped Shaw in his legal struggle with Garrison. This may explain why the governors of three states refused to honor Garrison's subpoenas.

Shaw's New Orleans-based International Trade Mart was connected to the shadowy European firm, Permindex, which was kicked out of France in 1962 on suspicion of involvment in the attempted assassination of French president Charles de Gaulle. Permindex's board of directors included von Braun and many well-known European fascists. Some experts say Permindex was a front for the postwar international Nazi underground known as the Odessa.

What can be done

That is far from an exhaustive list of the theories that have been put forward during the almost thirty years since Kennedy was assassinated. Perhaps the most plausible of them is that some elements of the Mongoose team and the Mafia pulled the job off together, with the involvement of people in other government agencies.

One thing, at least, is clear: the assassination must have been an inside job. Aside from all the anomalies in the government's behavior, how could outsiders have gotten away with it?

From day one, the government has acted as if it wanted the whole thing over and done with—and with the fewest possible disturbing implications. But it does not have to get its way. There are certain things we can demand of the government to help us find out what actually happened that Friday in Dallas.

- The acoustics evidence should be definitively assessed. Does it prove a fourth shot or not?

- Ballistics tests should—at long last—be run to determine whether the "magic bullet" theory is realistic.

- Photographic and film evidence of the grassy knoll should be analyzed by the most sophisticated means available.

- The JFK archives being kept secret until 2029 and 2039 should be unsealed—including the Lopez report that would seem to prove Oswald was impersonated in Mexico City during the fall of 1963.

- All the CIA and Defense Department files associated with Operation Mongoose, JM/Wave, Task Force W and all other operations aimed at overthrowing Castro during JFK's administration should be declassified.

- Some attempt should be made to determine the fate of the materials missing from the National Archives.

- Finally, a special prosecutor should appointed to stay with this case for as long as it takes to follow the trail of evidence to its end.

Many of these steps could be brought about with a stroke of the president's pen. They might not crack the case but at least they would open a door of hope that has been held closed too long by the forces of concealment and duplicity. The American people need such hope. Without it, it is hard to see how American democracy can survive.

Notes

*The author names and abbreviations below refer to the works listed the next section, **Works cited**.*

Chapter One

p. 5. 400 threats on JFK's life—Blakey, 6-9.
Democrats' theft of 1960 election—Blakey, 377.

p. 6. JFK's role in the Bay of Pigs—O'Donnell, 312.
"Splinter the CIA...to the winds"—*New York Times*, 5/25/66.

p. 6–7. JFK's CIA purge—Blakey, 55.

p. 7. Khrushchev's threat—Ranelagh, 393.

p. 8. JFK and Vietnam—Prouty, 406.

Chapter Two

p. 11–12. Katzenbach quote—HCA III, 675.

p. 12. Hoover quote—HCA IX, 3.

p. 14. Sequence of shots—WCR, 110-17.
Duration of gunfire—WCR, 117.

p. 15. Zapruder film—WCR, 43.   James Tague hit—WCR, 116.

p. 16. Oswald's behavior after the shooting—WCH III, 257.

p. 17. Description of Oswald on police radio—WCH XXIII, 916.
"We've had a shooting here...."—WCR, 164-65.

p. 18. Oswald's rifle found—WCR, 79.

p. 19. Oswald identified by Baker—WCH XXIV, 307.
LBJ sworn in—Miller, 148.
Oswald "very arrogant and argumentative"—WCH VII, 310.
Hosty's description of Oswald—WCH IV, 466.
Oswald's denials—WCH XXIV, 264.

p. 20. Oswald charged with Tippit murder—WCH IV, 468.
Oswald a "patsy"—WCR, 17.
Oswald charged with killing JFK—WCH XXIV, 270.
Incriminating photographs of Oswald—WCH VII, 315-17.

p. 21. Account of Oswald's shooting—WCR, 17.

p. 22. Ruby's denial—WCR, 17-18.
Public's response to Warren findings—MacFarlane, 10.

p. 22–23. Hosty's contacts with Oswald—Summers 370-72.

p. 23. CIA's assassination attempts—Ranelagh, 335-37.

p. 24. The Assassination Committee's findings—Blakey, 157-78.

Chapter Three

p. 26. Oswald's rifle—WCR, 97.

p. 27. Richard Russell's doubts—Weisburg, 21.
Cooper quote—Epstein 1, 122.
Hale Boggs' strong doubts—Epstein 1, 122.
"The medical evidence alone...."—HCA VII, 179.

p. 28. "[Connally] didn't immediately feel...."—WCR, 112, 115.
Shaw quote—WCH IV, 116.

p. 29. Clark quote—Shaw, 76.   Shaw quote—Shaw, 76.

p. 30. CE 399's pristine condition—WCR, 79.

p. 32. Bell quote—Summers, 546.   Harbison testimony—AIBP, 4-5/77.

p. 33. Connally quotes—*Life*, 11/25/66, 48. Also see WCR, 98-109.

p. 34–35. Witnesses' opinions on shots—Summers, 22-24.

p. 35. 1st Powers quote—WCH VII, 472.
1976 Powers quote—AIBM, 12/29/78, citing a TV interview by
    Steve Curwood of WGBH-TV, Boston.
Hargis quote—WCH VI 294-95.

p. 36. Newman quote—Summers, 23.   Arnold quote—Summers, 26
Holland quote—Summers, 28.   Winborn quote—AIBM, 12/29/78.

p. 36–37. Bowers quote—WCH VI, 288.

p. 38. Riddle quote—WCH VI, 294-95.
JFK's reaction to the head shot—HCR 173-74.

p. 39. Perry quote—Miller, 149.   Clark quote—HCA VI, 20.
McClelland quote—HCA VI, 33-35.

p. 41. O'Connor's description of casket—IR I.

p. 41–42. Autopsy discrepancies—Lifton, especially 100-111, 389,
600-601, photo 32 following 586, photo 3 following 682.

p. 42. Acoustics evidence—HCA, 65-78. Also see HCA V, 690-93.

p. 45-46. Barger quote—Summers, 475.

p. 46-47. Bowers quote—WCH VI, 288.

p. 47. Three tramps' identities—Canfield.

p. 48. Harrelson quote—Marrs, 333-36.   1988 Harrelson interview—IR I.
New info on tramp's identities—*Newsweek,* 12/23/91, p. 54.

p. 49. Milteer interview—Summers, 404.   Sapp quote—Summers, 234.

p. 50. Miami handbill—Summers, 234.
Arrests of Braden and Lawrence—Shaw, 85-86, 90.

p. 51. Aerospace Corp. photo enhancement—HCA VI, 122-25.

p. 51–52. Moorman photograph—IR II.

p. 53. Baker's and Truly's observations—Marrs, 50-53.

p. 54. FBI memo—Groden, 147.   Nitrate tests—Summers, 554.
Marina quote—WCH XXII, CE 1403, 778 and XXVI, CE 2694, 62-64.

p. 55. Tomlinson testimony—WCR, 81 and WCH VI, 126-34.
Second magic bullet—HCA VII, 116. Also see Lifton, 645-47.

p. 55–57. Oswald: the picture is a phony—WCR, 608-609.

p. 55–57. Other critics' views of Oswald photos—Meagher, 207;
Summers, 64-65.   Walker shooting—WCH XI, 410.

p. 58. Marina's testimony—WCH I, 16-17.
"Capacity for violence"—WCR, 20-23. Note for Marina—WCR, 184.
Oswald's motivation— WCR. 406.   Walker a "fascist."—WCR, 406.

p. 59. Police description of Walker bullet—Summers, 208.
Frazier and Nichol quote—WCR, 562.
Coleman testimony—WCH XXVI, 437-38.

p. 59–60. Walker house photos—Summers, plate 9.

p. 60–62. Tippit—Summers, 87-95, 346, 557. Also see Epstein 1, 109.

p. 63. Oswald in Mexico City—WCR, 375 and Summers, 346
Oswald's military activities—Melanson, 3; Summers, 146.
Hemming quote—Summers, 146, 268. CIA memo—AIBB, 6/4/77, 6.

p. 64. Oswald's activities in New Orleans—Davis, 13, 132.
Transcriptions and photographs of Oswald—Groden, 3-4.
Descriptions of Oswald and impersonator—Summers, 349, 357.

p. 66. Lopez quote—BBC. FBI memo—Melanson, 114.
1/20/61 impersonation—Garrison, 57-59.

p. 66–67. 9/25/63 impersonation—Melanson, 106.

p. 67. 10/63 impersonation—Blakey, 163.
11/1/63 impersonation—Melanson, 108
11/9/63 impersonation—Melanson, 107.

p. 68. Quality of Bronson film—HCR, 49.
Craig quote—WCR, 160-61; WCH VI, 265-67.
Leibeler quote—HCA XI, 226.

p. 69. Why Ruby shot Oswald—WCR, 374. Anonymous phone tips—IR V.

p. 69-70. Ruby's conversation with Warren & Ford—WCH V, 181-213.

p. 70. Ruby's past—Blakey, 279-339. Also see HCR, 149-56.
" Ruby entered...without assistance"—HCR, 157.
Ruby's death—Miller, 218.

p. 71–74. Underhill through Roselli—Marrs, 558-68;
Mohrenschildt, Nicoletti, Prio—Summers, 492-94.

Chapter Four

p. 76. Soviets-did-it theories—Epstein 2; Eddowes.

p. 77. Real job of Warren Commission—HCA XI, 7.

p. 78. Who's buried in Oswald's grave—Melanson, 3.

p. 79. Marcello threatens to have JFK killed—HCR, 171.

p. 80. Mafia attempts to kill Castro—HCA X, 179.
J. Edgar Hoover's involvment—North.

p. 80. Cowboys vs. Yankees—Buchanan; Oglesby.

p. 81. Anger of Texans—Groden, 26 ff.

p. 82. Gehlen Org in CIA—Reese

p. 83—CIA support of Shaw—Marchetti; Marrs.
Shaw and Permindex—Garrison; Marrs, 515.

Works cited
(and/or recommended)

*The names and abbreviations in **boldface** below
indicate how materials are referred to in the Notes.*

Assassination Information Bureau. *Memos* (**AIBM**), *Progress Reports* (**AIBP**) and *Briefing Documents* (**AIBB**), housed at the Assassination Archives and Research Center, Washington DC

BBC (British Broadcasting Corporation). TV special, *The Trial of Oswald*, 1988.

Blakey, G. Robert, and Richard N. Billings. *The Plot to Kill the President: Organized Crime Assassinated JFK*, Times Books, 1981.

Buchanan, Thomas G. *Who Killed Kennedy?*, G. P. Putnam's Sons, 1964.

Canfield, Michael and A.J. Weberman. *Coup d'Etat in America*, Third Press, 1975.

The Church Report (**CR**). *Senate Select Committee to Study Governmental Operations with Respect to Intelligence Activities, Final Report*, Government Printing Office, April 23, 1976.

Davis, John H. *Mafia Kingfish: Carlos Marcello and the Assassination of John F. Kennedy*. McGraw-Hill, 1989.

Eddowes, Michael. *Krushchev Killed Kennedy*, self-published, 1975.

Epstein, Edward Jay. **1.** *Inquest: The Warren Commission of the Establishment of Truth.* Viking Press, 1966.

   2. *Legend: The Secret World of Lee Harvey Oswald.* McGraw-Hill, 1978.

Fonzi, Gaeton. "Who Killed JFK?" *Washington Monthly,* November 1980.

Garrison, Jim. *On the Trail of the Assassins: My Investigation and Prosecution of the Murder of President Kennedy.* Sheridan Square Press, 1988.

Groden, Robert J., and Harrison Edward Livingstone. *High Treason, the Assassination of President John F. Kennedy: What Really Happened?* The Conservatory Press, 1989.

House Select Committee on Assassinations, Report (**HCR**) and *Investigation of the Assassination of President John F. Kennedy* (**HCA**), 11 volumes. Government Printing Office, 1979.

Investigative Reports (**IR**). Five-part series, *The Men Who Killed Kennedy.* First aired in the US on the Arts and Entertainment cable network, 1991. *(Some of the material in this series is speculative.)*

Joesten, Joachim. *Oswald: Assassin or Fall Guy?* Marzani and Munsel, 1964.

Kantor, Seth. *Who Was Jack Ruby?* Everest House, 1978.

Khrushchev, Nikita. *Khrushchev Remembers,* 2 vols. Little Brown, 1970, 1974.

Kirkwood, James. *American Grotesque: An Account of the Clay Shaw-Jim Garrison Affair in the City of New Orleans.* Simon and Schuster, 1970.

Lane, Mark. **1.** *Rush to Judgment: A Critique of the Warren Commission's Inquiry into the Murders of President John F. Kennedy, Officer J.D. Tippit and Lee Harvey Oswald.* Holt Rinehard Winston, 1966.

   2. *Plausible Denial: Was the CIA Involved in the Assassination of JFK?* Thunder's Mouth Press, 1991.

Lifton, David S. *Best Evidence: Disguise and Deception in the Assassination of John F. Kennedy.* Macmillan, 1980; paperback edition, Carroll & Graf, 1988.

MacFarlane, Ian. *Proof of Conspiracy.* Book Publishers, 1975.

Marchetti, Victor. *The CIA and the Cult of Intelligence.* Knopf, 1974.

Marrs, Jim. *Crossfire: The Plot that Killed Kennedy.* Carroll & Graf, 1989.

Meagher, Sylvia. *Accessories After the Fact: The Warren Commission, the Authorities and the Report,* 1967; republished with preface by Sen. Richard S. Schweiker and introduction by Peter Dale Scott, Vintage Books, 1976.

Melanson, Philip. *Spy Saga: Lee Harvey Oswald and US Intelligence.* Praeger, 1990.

Miller, Tom. *The Assassination Please Almanac.* Regnery, 1977.

Morrow, Robert D. *Betrayal: A reconstruction of certain clandestine events from the Bay of Pigs to the assassination of John Fitzgerald Kennedy.* Little Brown, 1972.

North, Mark. *Act of Treason: The Role of J. Edgar Hoover in the Assassination of President Kennedy,* Carroll & Graf, 1991.

O'Donnell, Kenneth P. and David F. Powers. *Johnny, We Hardly Knew Ye.* Pocket Books, 1973.

Oglesby, Carl. *The Yankee and Cowboy War.* Berkley Medallion, 1977.

Prouty, L. Fletcher. *The Secret Team.* Prentice Hall, 1973.

Ranelagh, John *The Agency,* Simon and Schuster, 1987.

Reese, Mary Ellen. *General Reinhard Gehlen: The CIA Connection,* George Mason University Press, 1990

Sauvage, Leo. *The Oswald Affair: An Examination of the Contradictions and Omissions of the Warren Report,* translated from the French by Charles Gaulkin. World Publishing Co., 1966.

Scheim, David E. *Contract On America: The Mafia Murder of President John F. Kennedy.* Shapolsky Publishers, 1988.

Scott, Peter Dale. *Crime and Cover-Up: The CIA, the Mafia, and the Dallas-Watergate Connection.* Westworks, 1977.

Shaw, Gary, with Larry R. Harris. *Cover-Up; The Governmental Conspiracy to Conceal the Facts About the Public Execution of John Kennedy.* Self-published, Cleburne, TX, 1976.

Summers, Anthony. *Conspiracy.* McGraw-Hill, 1980; updated and expanded edition, Paragon House, 1989.

Thompson, Josiah. *Six Seconds in Dallas: A Micro-Study of the Kennedy Assassination.* Random House, 1967.

Warren Commission Report (**WCR**), one volume, and *Hearings* (**WCH**), 26 volumes. Government Printing Office, 1964. (**CE** stands for Commission Exhibit.)

Weisburg, Harold. *Whitewash IV,* 1974

Index

The Real Story series is based on a simple idea—political books don't have to be boring. Short, well-written and to the point, Real Story books are meant to be <u>read</u>. (And they're just $5 each.)

If you liked this book, check out some of the others in the Real Story series:

Who Owns the US? • Gore Vidal

Vidal is one of our country's most important (and witty) writers, and this is the clearest, most accessible summary ever of his political views.   *Winter, 1991-92*

What Uncle Sam Really Wants • Noam Chomsky

A brilliant analysis of the real motivations behind US foreign policy, from one of America's most popular speakers. Very clear and readable.   *Winter, 1991-92*

Burma—the Next Killing Fields? • Alan Clements

If we don't do something, Burma will become another Cambodia. Written by one of the few Westerners ever to have lived there, this book tells the story vividly.

Spring, 1992

Real Story books are available at most good bookstores, or send $5 per book + $2 shipping per order to Odonian Press, Box 7776, Berkeley CA 94707. For information on quantity discounts, please write or call us at 510/524-3143.